What Readers Are Saying About *iPad Programming*

iPad Programming is a great resource for iPhone developers to immerse themselves in the new world of iPad development. Whether creating new iPad apps or universal apps for both iPhone and iPad, this book covers essential user interface and development topics specific to the iPad that enable both beginning and more advanced iPhone developers to participate in this exciting iPad application market.

► **Raven Zachary**
Founder of iPhoneDevCamp and iPadDevCamp, President, Small Society

A must-read for software developers planning to create new iPad apps or looking forward to porting existing iPhone apps into this new device. Eric and Daniel don't merely enumerate classes and methods in this book but rather introduce each new feature of the 3.2 SDK with great detail, all in the context of the most important element of any iOS app: the user experience. This book helps developers build apps not only that are fast and stable but that leverage all the magic features of the iPad.

► **Adrian Kosmaczewski**
Director, akosma software

iPad Programming includes some incredible gems and details that you won't find elsewhere. It has become my go-to reference for gestures, video, and custom controls over video and with keyboards.

► **Joseph Heck**
Founder, Seattle Xcoders SIG

This book hits the sweet spot: it doesn't cover all the ground of a beginning iPhone programming book, but it doesn't require you to be an expert, either. Anyone who has mastered the basics of iPhone development and wants to include the iPad in their repertoire will learn something from this book and have fun doing it. I know I will be using this book as a reference for my next development project.

▶ **Janine Sisk**
Trial by Fyre Software, LLC

As an iPhone developer, getting involved with iPad development was a natural and mandatory step. Coming into this book, I was expecting only a technical document describing the "how to" for this or that. I was quite pleased, however, to discover the change in its tone. That tone let me see the iPad from the nondeveloper perspective. I began to see what it actually "is," and what it's capable of. This book will be referenced often.

▶ **Kevin J. Garriott**
Senior Developer, Mobile Applications, Rockfish Interactive

iPad Programming

A Quick-Start Guide for iPhone Developers

iPad Programming

A Quick-Start Guide for iPhone Developers

Daniel H Steinberg

Eric T Freeman

The Pragmatic Bookshelf

Raleigh, North Carolina   Dallas, Texas

Many of the designations used by manufacturers and sellers to distinguish their products are claimed as trademarks. Where those designations appear in this book, and The Pragmatic Programmers, LLC was aware of a trademark claim, the designations have been printed in initial capital letters or in all capitals. The Pragmatic Starter Kit, The Pragmatic Programmer, Pragmatic Programming, Pragmatic Bookshelf and the linking *g* device are trademarks of The Pragmatic Programmers, LLC.

Every precaution was taken in the preparation of this book. However, the publisher assumes no responsibility for errors or omissions, or for damages that may result from the use of information (including program listings) contained herein.

Our Pragmatic courses, workshops, and other products can help you and your team create better software and have more fun. For more information, as well as the latest Pragmatic titles, please visit us at http://www.pragprog.com.

The team that produced this book includes:

Editor: Colleen Toporek
Indexing: Sara Eastler
Copy edit: Kim Wimpsett
Layout: Steve Peter
Production: Janet Furlow
Customer support: Ellie Callahan
International: Juliet Benda

ISBN-10: 1-934356-57-3

ISBN-13: 978-1-934356-57-9

Printed on acid-free paper.

P1.0 printing, September 2010

Version: 2010-9-15

Contents

Chapter 1

From iPhone to iPad

Before you write a line of code for your iPad app, you need to hold the device in your hands. You need to feel the device melt away as you become immersed in an app. The app you are using gets out of your way as you get involved in an activity it enables.

That's the kind of app we want you to write.

We don't merely want you to write apps that run on an iPad; we want you to write apps that are perfect for the platform. People are going to tell their friends about your app because it delights them when they notice it, and it disappears as they use it.

How can that be? Isn't the iPad just an oversized iPod touch that runs on the same iOS we already know and love?[1] Have we become caught up in the marketing hype generated by Steve Jobs' famous reality distortion field?

No. There is something fundamentally different about this high-resolution device with its large display that fits in your hands but not your pocket—a device that you navigate with Multi-Touch and gestures.

Throughout this book, we show you how to build experiences for this new device. We'll explore the similarities and differences between developing for the iPad and what you're used to in developing for the iPhone. We aren't presenting a single, unified example that displays everything at once. We'll look at individual topics and leave it to you to decide when and how to use them in the applications you are building.

---

1. At WWDC 2010, the operating system previously known as iPhone OS was rebranded as iOS. At this time, the operating system is referred to as iOS, while the developer APIs are still branded iPhone SDK.

We'll begin in the world that you know. We'll start by creating an iPhone app in this chapter and transform it into an app that runs on your iPad.

But first let's figure out how the iPad fits in your end users' lives—somewhere between the laptop and the iPhone.

1.1 The iPad and the Laptop

Once you've checked email or surfed the Web on an iPad, your laptop is going to seem bulkier and less portable than it was the minute before you picked up the iPad. Suddenly, you'll be aware of the amount of space required to house the keyboard, trackpad, hard drive, and battery.

On the other hand, your iPad is more constrained. It is not meant to live as a stand-alone device. It must be synced to a laptop or desktop machine once in a while. It doesn't have the processing power, memory, or storage of a laptop. It is designed to belong to a single user, with a single app occupying your attention at any given time. The iPad is not meant to be the digital hub that a desktop or laptop becomes. For now, it is a node on the hub, not the center of your digital universe.

Most importantly, there is something very different about interacting with the screen by touching it as opposed to having to use a mouse or a trackpad. On the iPad, you use your finger to land planes in Flight Control, paint beautiful images with Brushes, and mark email messages as deleted. If you want to move or guide an object, you put your finger on it and move your finger. The object comes along for the ride.

If you want to resize an object, you use two fingers to pinch or zoom. You use your finger to resize, reposition, and crop an image. You zoom in on a web page to better read it and so that your finger can more easily select the right text box to type into. These gestures have become so natural that it feels strange to use a mouse to select an object and grab handles to resize and reposition. Reaching for the mouse or the trackpad takes us out of the moment.

The last important difference between an iPad and a laptop is that you can easily rotate the iPad 90 degrees and get a whole different view of your application. In fact, as an iPad developer, you are asked to consider how best to present your app in both landscape and portrait orientations.

What About iOS 4?

At its launch, the iPad ran iPhone OS 3.2, which added many APIs and techniques to iPhone OS 3. Apple released iOS 4 for iPhone in June 2010. Many of the topics covered in this book will help you take advantage of new features in iOS4. For example, the new gesture APIs introduced for the iPad are now available on iOS 4.

So, the question about iOS 4 can be a bit confusing. A lot of the new APIs introduced for the iPad in iPhone 3.2 are part of iOS 4. So if you are writing iOS 4 apps for the iPhone, then the relevant sections of this book will be helpful. There are, however, some features that are new to iOS 4 and are not yet available for the iPad. Multitasking, for example, is not part of iPhone 3.2 and is not covered by this book. iOS 4 will not be available on the iPad until well after this book is completed.

1.2 The iPad and the iPod Touch

Much of the GUI that you know and love on Mac OS X and later on Windows originated at Xerox PARC with Alan Kay's team. Kay has consistently complained that the way we interact with a computer has not changed enough from the work his team was doing decades ago. Alan Kay told Gigaom's Janko Roettgers this story about Kay's reaction to the unveiling of the iPhone in 2007.

"When the Mac first came out, *Newsweek* asked me what I [thought] of it. I said, 'Well, it's the first personal computer worth criticizing.' So, at the end of the [iPhone] presentation, Steve came up to me and said, 'Is the iPhone worth criticizing?' And I said, 'Make the screen five inches by eight inches, and you'll rule the world.'"[2]

So, isn't that what the iPad is? Isn't the iPad *just* a big iPod touch?

It's certainly true that the iPad runs iOS. That's exactly the same operating system that runs on the iPhone and the iPod touch. In fact, you will use many of the same APIs when you write your iPad apps that you use to write apps for the iPhone.

---

2. http://gigaom.com/2010/01/26/alan-kay-with-the-tablet-apple-will-rule-the-world/

It's also true that an iPad is much bigger than an iPhone. An iPad is about the size of the printed version of this book—about half an inch taller and a little thinner but roughly the same size. The iPhone is much smaller. Here's a picture that shows the relative size of two iPhone screens to the iPad screen:

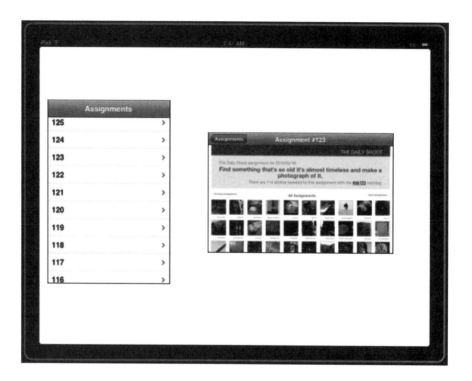

So, the iPad *is* a big iPod touch—but it's not *just* a big iPod touch. Being bigger is the key to what makes it special.

The size is an important part of the story. On the iPad, you can browse web pages at full resolution, sort your pictures into piles with a flick of your finger, and fill out forms using a keyboard that you can fit all of your fingers on.

You will be missing the point if you think of the iPad from the developer's point of view. The APIs are similar enough to those for the iPhone that apps for one device can easily be run on the other. When you start to create an app for the iPad, take the time to understand what is different and special about this device.

What You Need for This Book

You will need to register as an iPhone developer for free at http://developer.apple.com/iphone. There is an additional yearly charge (currently $99) if you want to deploy your applications to your iPad or iPhone or sell your applications on the iTunes App Store.

Some of the material in this book such as file sharing and using external displays will require that you are running the example on the device.

Once you've registered, download the latest tools and SDKs. Currently, iPad development requires that you are running Mac OS X 10.6.2 on an Intel machine. The examples in this book were created using Xcode version 3.2.3 and iPhone SDK 3.2. We assume that you are using the modern simulator that was first shipped as part of Xcode 3.2.3.

Also, you can download all the projects for this book from the book's home page at http://pragprog.com/titles/sfipad. We have staged the projects so that you can follow along or pick them up at a certain point to compare your work to ours.

The templates supplied by Apple keep changing, so you should expect to see small differences now and then.

Your favorite iPhone apps are the ones that take advantage of all the capabilities of the iPhone in natural ways.[3] They incorporate the accelerometer, the compass, the GPS, the camera, and the phone itself when it makes sense. In the remainder of the book, we will show you *how* to program the iPad, but it's up to you to think about *what* to program.

---

3. It will get tedious to say "iPhone and iPod touch" every time. We'll often use one or the other to refer to the common platform.

1.3 Getting Started

In this book, we assume you know how to develop iPhone apps. Maybe you've written an iPhone app or two for fun or profit. You are certainly familiar with Cocoa, Objective-C, and the iPhone APIs. You are comfortable with the most recent versions of Xcode and Interface Builder. You know how to work with view controllers and delegates and can use reference counting to manage memory.

That's where we'll start.

We'll create an iPhone app and quickly review some of the key concepts you'll need to know in this book. These techniques are common to iPhone and iPad development. You'll see this at the end of the chapter when we convert this from a project that works only on the iPhone to one that works on both the iPhone and the iPad.

By the end of this chapter, you'll know whether you have the right amount of background for this book. Everything should be familiar, and the quick review should be enough to bring you up to speed for the remainder of the book. If you find yourself confused or think we're moving too fast, then you may need to start with a book on Cocoa or iPhone development.[4]

If you think we're moving too slowly and you want to get right to the iPad material, start with the project in the FromTo/DailyShoot1 directory in the code download, and skip ahead to Section 1.8, *Compatibility Mode*.

We'll build a simple navigation-based application around The Daily Shoot website (http://dailyshoot.com) created by Mike Clark and James Duncan Davidson. Their site has suggested a daily assignment for photographers since November 2009. In this type of app, users navigate through some number of levels of table views until they select an individual item and navigate to its detail view.

---

4. You can start with *Cocoa Programming: A Quick-Start Guide for Developers* [Ste09] and/or *iPhone SDK Development* [DA09].

Disappearing ivars

If you've been programming for the iPhone for a while, then you're probably used to a rhythm when declaring properties. You declare an ivar and the corresponding property in the header file, synthesize the property, and release it in the implementation file.

Now with the new simulator released with Xcode 3.2.3, you no longer have to declare the ivar. The instance variable will be synthesized by the runtime in the simulator just as it has been on the device all along. Soon you also won't have to explicitly synthesize the property once "synthesize by default" is available as a compiler option.

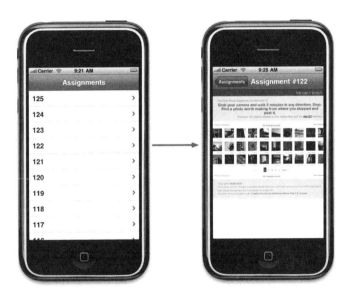

Our app will launch with a simple table that is filled with the numbers of the first 125 assignments. When a user selects a number, we will display the landing page for that assignment.

There's nothing fancy about this example, but it lets us set up all of the machinery we need for a navigation-based application, and it sets the stage for the split view–based application in the next chapter.

Start Xcode, and create a new navigation-based application that does *not* use Core Data for storage. Name the project DailyShoot.

By the way, you may have noticed some important differences in the templates you have available. The Split View-based Application template is new and can be used only for iPad-based projects. The Navigation-based Application and Utility Application templates can be used only for new iPhone projects. The Window-based template can create an iPhone project, an iPad project, or a universal project that targets both platforms at once. The remaining templates can be used as the starting point for either iPhone or iPad projects, but you have to specify which using a drop-down.

We're not going to do anything with the app delegate or with the Main-Window nib. If this were a production app, we would take the time to change the name of the RootViewController class and the corresponding nib to something that has more meaning in the current setting. Because it's easy to make an error while making these changes and because the changes have nothing to do with what we're working on in this chapter, we'll leave the names as they are.

1.4 Adding a Model Object

A table view needs a data source that can answer three basic questions:

- How many sections are in the table?
- For each section, how many rows are in this section?
- For each row, what goes in this row?

In the project created for us from the template, the RootViewController is the table view's data source. We're going to add a model object to our project. This is the classic Model View Controller (MVC) decoupling. The view talks to the controller and the controller talks to the model.

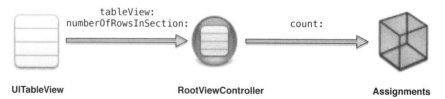

UITableView   RootViewController   Assignments

The table view sends the message tableView:numberOfRowsInSection: to the controller. The controller in turn sends the message count to the Assignments object, our model object. The model object responds to the controller with the number of assignments, which the controller then relays to the table view so that it knows how many rows will be displayed.

To implement this, in Xcode add a new Objective-C class that is a subclass of NSObject and name it Assignments.

An Assignments object will need to let the controller know how many total assignments there are and be able to tell the controller which assignment number goes in a given row. It will keep the collection of assignments internally in an NSArray named assignmentArray. This is all captured in the header file:

FromTo/DailyShoot1/Classes/Assignments.h

```
#import <Foundation/Foundation.h>

@interface Assignments : NSObject {
    NSArray *assignmentArray;
}
-(NSUInteger) count;
-(NSNumber *) assignmentAtIndex:(NSUInteger) index;
@end
```

There's not much to our implementation. The count and assignmentAtIndex: methods do little more than relay information from the assignmentArray. The other methods create and release the array.

FromTo/DailyShoot1/Classes/Assignments.m

```
#import "Assignments.h"

@implementation Assignments
-(NSUInteger) count {
    return [assignmentArray count];
}
-(NSNumber *) assignmentAtIndex:(NSUInteger) index {
    return [assignmentArray objectAtIndex:index];
}
-(void) awakeFromNib {
    NSMutableArray *temp = [NSMutableArray array];
    for (int i = 0; i < 125; i++) {
        [temp addObject:[NSNumber numberWithInt:125 - i]];
    }
    assignmentArray = [[NSArray alloc] initWithArray:temp];
}
-(void) dealloc {
    [assignmentArray release], assignmentArray = nil;
    [super dealloc];
}
@end
```

Save your work, and open RootViewController.xib in IB. Select the Classes tab of the Library, and find the Assignments class that we just created. Drag it into the Document window to create an instance of Assignments. Save.

The model object is now complete. Let's connect it to the controller.

1.5 The *C* in MVC

The RootViewController needs to communicate with the model object we just created. They both are instantiated in the same nib, so we can easily connect them. Add a property of type Assignments in RootViewController.h, and declare it to be an outlet.

FromTo/DailyShoot1/Classes/RootViewController.h

```
#import <UIKit/UIKit.h>
▶ @class Assignments;

@interface RootViewController : UITableViewController {
}
▶ @property(nonatomic, retain) IBOutlet Assignments *assignments;
@end
```

Save the header file, and jump over to IB to connect the outlet to the Assignments object in RootViewController.xib. Save your work in IB.

Import Assignments.h at the top of RootViewController.m, and synthesize the assignments variable. Set the table view's title to Assignments in viewDidLoad, and return YES from the method shouldAutorotateToInterfaceOrientation:.

FromTo/DailyShoot1/Classes/RootViewController.m

```
#import "RootViewController.h"
#import "Assignments.h"
#import "AssignmentViewController.h"

@implementation RootViewController
@synthesize assignments;
- (void)viewDidLoad {
    [super viewDidLoad];
    self.title = @"Assignments";
}
- (BOOL)shouldAutorotateToInterfaceOrientation:
(UIInterfaceOrientation)interfaceOrientation {
        return YES;
}
```

You'll need to make the following highlighted changes to the data source methods:

FromTo/DailyShoot1/Classes/RootViewController.m

```
- (NSInteger)numberOfSectionsInTableView:(UITableView *)tableView {
    return 1;
}
- (NSInteger)tableView:(UITableView *)tableView
 numberOfRowsInSection:(NSInteger)section {
►    return [self.assignments count];
}
- (UITableViewCell *)tableView:(UITableView *)tableView
        cellForRowAtIndexPath:(NSIndexPath *)indexPath {

    static NSString *CellIdentifier = @"Cell";

    UITableViewCell *cell =
    [tableView dequeueReusableCellWithIdentifier:CellIdentifier];
    if (cell == nil) {
        cell = [[[UITableViewCell alloc]
                initWithStyle:UITableViewCellStyleDefault
                reuseIdentifier:CellIdentifier] autorelease];
►        cell.accessoryType = UITableViewCellAccessoryDisclosureIndicator;
    }
►    cell.textLabel.text =
►        [[self.assignments assignmentAtIndex:indexPath.row] stringValue];

    return cell;
}
```

That's not a lot of code to add. Build and run, and the application should build and launch; you should see the assignment numbers in decreasing order in the table view. We're halfway there.

1.6 The Detail View and Its Controller

When our end user selects an assignment number in the table view, we're going to reveal a new view containing a web view with the assignment's landing page. We'll need to implement the delegate method table-View:didSelectRowAtIndexPath: so that it creates a view controller to control this view, and then we need to push the view controller onto the stack managed by the navigation controller.

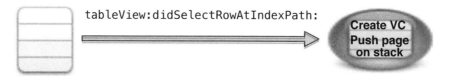

UITableView   **RootViewController**

In this section, we'll create the view controller and its associated nib. In the next section, we'll implement the delegate method.

Create a new UIViewController subclass, selecting only the "With XIB for user interface" option. Name it AssignmentViewController. You'll find it easier to manage if you move the nib file to the Resources group and leave the source code in the Classes group.

The AssignmentViewController will need an outlet to communicate with its web view and a property so that the RootViewController can pass in the assignment number that corresponds to the row the user selects.

FromTo/DailyShoot1/Classes/AssignmentViewController.h

```
#import <UIKit/UIKit.h>

@interface AssignmentViewController : UIViewController {
}
@property (nonatomic, retain) IBOutlet UIWebView *webView;
@property (nonatomic, retain) NSNumber *assignmentNumber;
@end
```

Double-click the AssignmentViewController nib file to open it with IB. Use the Attributes inspector to set the view's top bar to Navigation Bar. Add a web view as a subview to the view, and resize it so it occupies all of the remaining space on the view. Select the Scale Pages To Fit box in the Attributes inspector for the web view. Connect the AssignmentView-Controller's webView outlet to the web view. Save. You can quit IB.

To implement the AssignmentViewController class, synthesize the variables, load the right URL, and set the title for the page in the view-DidLoad method.

FromTo/DailyShoot1/Classes/AssignmentViewController.m

```
@synthesize webView, assignmentNumber;

- (void) loadSelectedPage {
  NSString *url =
    [NSString stringWithFormat:@"http://dailyshoot.com/assignments/%@",
                          self.assignmentNumber];
```

```
    [self.webView loadRequest:
      [NSURLRequest requestWithURL:[NSURL URLWithString:url]]];
}
-(void)viewDidLoad {
    [super viewDidLoad];
    self.title = [NSString stringWithFormat:@"Assignment #%@",
                 self.assignmentNumber];
    [self loadSelectedPage];
}
```

At this point, you have the view controller ready to be pushed onto the stack along with the view it controls; also implement the shouldAutoRotateToInterfaceOrientation: method to return YES..

1.7 Implementing the Table Delegate Method

A table view has both a data source and a delegate. We've already implemented the required data source methods in the RootViewController. These are the methods that tell the table view what it needs to display.

The delegate methods are responsible for responding to user interaction with the table. In particular, when a user selects an assignment, the delegate method tableView:didSelectRowAtIndexPath: is called. In this navigation-based example, the RootViewController is the delegate for the table view. You'll see in the next chapter that this won't always be the case.

Most of the tableView:didSelectRowAtIndexPath: method is stubbed out for you in RootViewController.m. All we need to change is the name of the controller class and the nib being loaded to AssignmentViewController. We also need to set the value of the assignmentNumber property to the number displayed in the row that the user has selected before we push the view controller.

FromTo/DailyShoot1/Classes/RootViewController.m

```
- (void)tableView:(UITableView *)tableView
didSelectRowAtIndexPath:(NSIndexPath *)indexPath {
    AssignmentViewController *detailViewController =
    [[AssignmentViewController alloc]
              initWithNibName:@"AssignmentViewController" bundle:nil];
    detailViewController.assignmentNumber =
                  [self.assignments assignmentAtIndex:indexPath.row];
    [self.navigationController pushViewController:detailViewController
                                        animated:YES];
    [detailViewController release];
}
```

Don't forget to import AssignmentViewController.h. Now when you build and run, everything should work.

We're done with our iPhone app. This is a good chance for you to take stock of where you are. We've worked with nibs, set outlets, implemented an example of the MVC pattern, used delegate methods, and changed what's on the screen by creating a new view controller and a nib that has it as its File's Owner. If you had no trouble keeping up with this example, you're in good shape for this introduction to programming the iPad.

In fact, it's time for us to transition this project from an iPhone-only project to a project that works on both platforms.

1.8 Compatibility Mode

This app we've just created will run on the iPad in compatibility mode. It is *not* an iPad app at this point—it is an iPhone app that we can run on an iPad. To view this in your simulator, we're going to need to make a small change to the project settings.

Choose the menu item Project > Edit Project Settings..., and select the Build tab. Assuming that you are using Xcode 3.2.3 or newer, Base SDK and iPhone OS Deployment Target are both set to iPhone 4.0. At the time of this writing, iPhone SDK 4.0 is not available for the iPad. You'll need to use the drop-down menu to change the iPhone OS Deployment target to iPhone OS 3.2.

Now you can run the DailyShoot app in the iPad simulator. In the Project menu, make sure Set Active SDK is set to Simulator and Set Active Executable is set to Daily Shoot - iPad Simulator 3.2. Run it, and the iPad simulator should launch.[5]

---

5. Many of the iPad screenshots are presented after rotating to landscape mode to save space.

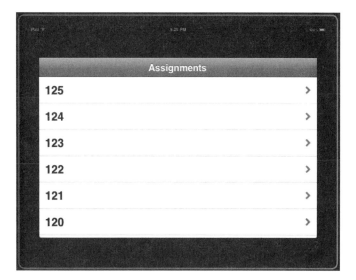

That's pretty nice. Apple has provided an easy way for iPhone apps to run on the iPad without requiring any changes from developers. This compatibility mode is a convenience for developers, not one you should ever rely on. On the iPad, an iPhone app can be viewed at its original size. Also, just as on the device, you can click the 2x round button in the lower-right corner of your simulator to view the app at twice its original size.

The good news is that this brings a ton of existing iPhone apps to the iPad, which allowed the new device to debut with a wide array of offerings. The bad news is that the look of these automatically adjusted apps isn't sharp. One pixel becomes four—two in each direction. It will be difficult to see the pixelation in these screenshots, but you can see them immediately in the simulator and on the device.

So, without doing any work, your iPhone app runs on an iPad. Our next step doesn't require much work and results in an app that takes advantage of the full screen of the iPad in full resolution.

1.9 Converting to a Universal Application

Right now you have an iPhone app. Sure, you've seen it can run on both the iPhone and the iPad, but it doesn't look native on the iPad. Even if your users aren't bothered by the fuzziness, they probably notice that your app doesn't take up all of their screen. This is in part because the aspect ratios of the iPhone and iPad are different.

If you are explicitly developing for both the iPhone and the iPad, you have three basic choices:

- You can create a universal application from a single target in a single project. This will produce a binary file that will run the iPhone version on the iPhone and run the iPad version on the iPad. The user buys and downloads a single application, and it behaves differently depending on the device onto which it is installed. If you are essentially writing the same application for both platforms, you should prefer this approach.

- If the iPhone and iPad applications are different from a user's perspective but share a lot of code, you should produce two binaries. In other words, you will have one project with two targets.

- If the iPhone and iPad applications are different from a user's perspective and they don't share any files, then you may want to create two distinct projects. This is the least preferred option.

We're going to choose the first option and turn our iPhone application into a universal application so that it can run on an iPad or an iPhone. For now, we're going to run the exact same application on both platforms. In the next chapter, you'll see how to change the look and feel on each platform.

In Xcode, select the target named DailyShoot, right-click it, and select "Upgrade current target for iPad."

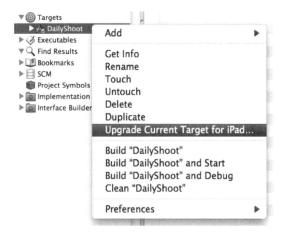

You can also find this option as a menu item in the Project menu.

Whichever path you take, you'll be given the choice of creating a single, universal application or two device-specific applications. Choose to create one universal application, and click the OK button.

There are two small visible changes. You should see that a new group has been created to hold your iPad resources, and it contains a new nib file.

Double-click the MainWindow-iPad nib to open it in IB, and you'll see that its structure is identical to the MainWindow nib. The dimensions of the window are different.

Now when you build and run the application as an iPad application, the app fills the entire screen, and the resolution is the same as the original iPhone native app.

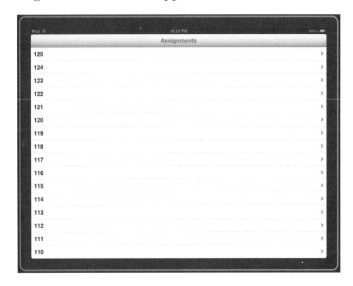

Wow. That looks terrible. Look at all that wasted space. If you select any of the assignments, then the detail page looks great. You'll see the browser in full size and resolution. But you can see from this example why there is no template for you to create a navigation-based iPad

---

Check MainWindow-iPad

Sometimes the upgrade to a universal app doesn't work correctly. You should check that the resulting nib is, in fact, an iPad window nib and not an iPhone nib. Double-click the Window object inside the nib, and a window will open containing this object. If it is the size of an iPhone window, then you need to upgrade the nib. Select the Document window, and choose the menu item File > Create iPad Version. You'll need to delete the iPhone version and save the iPad version as MainWindow-iPad.xib.

---

app for the iPad. In the next chapter, we'll use a split view to fix this problem.

1.10 Adding Little Touches

There are a few little tweaks we should make before continuing. The app icon for the iPad is 72×72px, whereas the iPhone icon size is 57×57px. Similarly, there are differences in the splash screens that are displayed at launch. For one thing, we're going to need to provide different screens depending on whether the app is launched in portrait or landscape. Finally, we need to make sure that the user can launch the application in landscape.

We haven't created an icon or a splash screen for the iPhone version of our application yet, so we'll take care of both the iPhone and iPad versions at once. Unless you are truly gifted as a designer and want to spend part of your development time doing design, you should find a designer to work with on your application. iPad owners expect their applications to be well designed. Bad design decisions make your users notice your app in ways that you wish they wouldn't.

Separate Icons

Let's create two simple icons for our application. You can use whatever you like. Compose an image with a camera in it or something that captures the idea behind the Daily Shoot app. We've created a simple icon by taking a screenshot of part of the book cover for this book and saving it as a PNG. You'll need to save your image in two different sizes. Name the iPhone version icon.png, and make sure it is 57×57 pixels. Name the iPad version icon-ipad.png, and make sure it is 72×72 pixels.

Drag these two PNG files under the Resources group in your Xcode project. When prompted, choose "Copy items into destination group's folder (if needed)."

Open DailyShoot-Info.plist in a text editor, and replace the item with the key CFBundleIconFile with the following item:[6]

```
<key>CFBundleIconFiles</key>
<array>
    <string>icon.png</string>
    <string>icon-ipad.png</string>
</array>
```

Clean your target, quit the simulator, and then build and run, and you will see the proper app icons. Here it is on the Dock with some of the icons for apps that Apple provides:

Apple also recommends that you create a 50×50 pixel icon and call it Icon-Small-50.png to be used by Spotlight on the iPad, as well as a 29×29 pixel icon named Icon-Small.png to be used by Spotlight on the iPhone. These icons are required if you are using Settings. We aren't going to add these icons, but if you would like, make sure you add them to the CFBundleIconFiles array in the plist as well.

Splash Screens

Our application launches quickly enough that we wouldn't normally need a splash screen. Let's create one anyway to see how it is done.

Make some simple splash screens for the app. They could be as simple as an image of the opening screen. For our example, we're using the string "The Daily Shoot" using the colors from the website.

This time we need to create three different files. Set the size for the splash screen for the iPhone app to be 320 pixels wide by 460 pixels

---

6. You can, of course, also use the plist editor to make this addition, but it's easier to show you what to do in code.

high, and save it as Default.png.[7] For the iPad, we need a portrait version at 768×1004 pixels saved as Default-Portrait.png and a landscape version at 1024×748 pixels named Default-Landscape.png.

Drag these three files into the Resources group so that your splash screens can appear at start-up.

Supporting Multiple Orientations at Start-Up

Once it's running, we make sure that our app can run in any orientation by returning YES from shouldAutorotateToInterfaceOrientation: in each of our view controllers. However, if you want to be able to *start* the app in any orientation, you have to add this element to DailyShoot-Info.plist:

```
<key>UISupportedInterfaceOrientations~ipad</key>
<array>
    <string>UIInterfaceOrientationPortrait</string>
    <string>UIInterfaceOrientationPortraitUpsideDown</string>
    <string>UIInterfaceOrientationLandscapeLeft</string>
    <string>UIInterfaceOrientationLandscapeRight</string>
</array>
```

iPhone apps always start in portrait orientation. By adding supported interface orientations to the plist, you are enabling your iPad app to start up in any of the orientations you include.

It is simple to add custom icons, launch screens, and additional orientations. These little touches will make a big difference to your end users. We now have launch screens and icons for both devices, and we've set the app to launch in any orientation on the iPad.

---

7. If you also want to target the new iPhone 4 and its Retina display, you will need a splash screen that is 640 pixels wide by 920 pixels high saved as Default@2x.png. Those details aren't relevant for our purposes.

1.11 Summary

As iPhone and iPad developers, we explicitly do *not* embrace the idea of "write once, run anywhere."[8] We will take advantage of a common code base when we can, but our design and development decisions will be driven by providing the most value for a specific user trying to accomplish a specific task on a specific device.

The universal version of our app doesn't make optimal use of the iPad. It still is built for the iPhone and tweaked to look OK on the iPad. As a thought experiment, let's make a few small adjustments to the image we used back in the beginning to compare the sizes of the iPhone and iPad screens to create an app that works like the iPhone app but takes advantage of the additional real estate of the iPad.

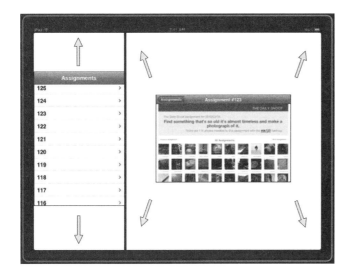

On the iPad in landscape mode, we can display both the navigation view and the browser at the same time. Imagine that we stretch the nav view to take the left side of the screen and grow the browser to fill the rest. This is exactly what we'll get in the next chapter when we use the split view.

What about in portrait mode?

---

8. This was the core value proposition of writing applications in the Java programming language.

You can see that we can't even fit the original iPhone screens on the iPad screen in this orientation. If we stretch them vertically, the combination would look crowded and distorted. That's why in portrait mode, the split view will show only the browser and not the navigation. Follow Apple's lead, and really work on all aspects of your interface for each device.

On the other hand, we've hit the ground running. You've already created a universal application that runs on the iPhone and iPad. In the process, we reviewed some of the core concepts common to programming for both devices using the iPhone SDK. You can read more about creating universal applications and the various plist properties you can set in Apple's *iPad Programming Guide* [App10b]. Now let's start working with an iPad-specific widget: the UISplitViewController.

Chapter 2

Introducing Split Views

This chapter is all about creating an app that feels as if it were designed for the iPad. We'll use two iPad-specific controllers: the UISplitViewController and the UIPopoverController.

The split view controller lets us combine the navigation and the detail view in one integrated screen. In this chapter, you're going to use the split view controller to present the navigation and detail view at the same time.

This works great when the user is holding the iPad horizontally, but it would look horrible if the user rotated the device and held it vertically. As you saw in the previous chapter, there just isn't enough room to show both panes at once.

The answer is to slide the navigation view out of sight and just display the detail view. If the users need to access the navigation, they can rotate the iPad, or they can press a button and bring up a new floating menu called a *popover*.

Here's the plan.

We're going to introduce a split view controller to the iPad version of our app. Remember that this is a universal application. As we work on the iPad version, our iPhone version must continue to work the way it currently does. If we were solely targeting the iPad, we would begin a new project with the Split View-based Application template. You'll find that left as an exercise at the end of this chapter.

In any case, once we have the split view controller up and running, the app will look right when it is launched in either orientation, but it won't behave correctly in either case. To make the landscape view work correctly, we're going to have to communicate between the navigation view and the detail view so that when the user selects an assignment in the navigation view, the web page corresponding to that assignment is loaded in the detail view. To make the portrait view work correctly, we're going to have to introduce a popover view that displays the assignments when the user needs them and dismisses the popover when the user doesn't need them anymore.

2.1 Introducing the Split View Controller in IB

In an iPhone navigation-based application, you present the user with a table view. When the user selects one of the rows, you either navigate to another table view or present them with a detail view of the item they selected. Because of the size constraints of the iPhone, each view is drawn on top of the previous view.

The analog on the iPad is the split view–based application. In landscape, the table view appears on the left. As the users select one of the rows, either you still navigate to another table view or you present them with the detail view of the item they selected. The difference is that if they are navigating to another table view, it will be presented in the left portion of the screen, and if they select an item, then the detail view, which is always visible on the right side of the screen, will update. In other words, the detail view changes when the users interact with it or when they navigate to a different selection.

Open the MainWindow-iPad nib.

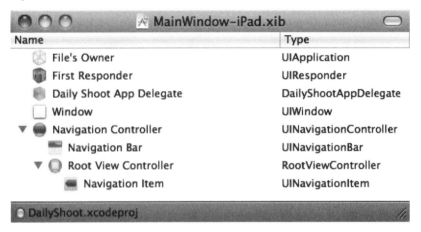

The Document window currently looks just like the Document window for the MainWindow nib that is used in the iPhone version. We'll change that now. Select the navigation controller, and delete it either using the delete key or using the menu item Edit > Delete. Find the split view controller in the Library, and drag it into the Document window where the navigation controller used to be.[1]

Open the disclosure triangles, and you'll see that the split view controller contains two controllers: a navigation controller and a view controller. We need to make some adjustments to make sure we're loading our custom classes.

---

1. If you don't find the split view controller on the Objects tab in the Library, your nib is an iPhone nib and not an iPad nib. Select your Document window, choose the menu option File > Create iPad Version, and replace the existing MainWindow-iPad.xib file with this newly created one.

Select the view controller, and use the Identity inspector to change its class to AssignmentViewController. While you're there, use the Attributes inspector to set the NIB name to the AssignmentViewController nib. Similarly, select Table View Controller under the navigation controller. Use the Identity inspector to change its type to RootViewController, and use the Attributes inspector to set its NIB name to RootViewController as well.

We need to fix a connection we broke when we deleted the original navigation controller. Select the app delegate, and use the Connections inspector to reconnect the navigationController outlet to the new navigation controller. Save your work. Build and run.

Surprised? The app runs exactly the same as it did at the end of the previous chapter. Where's our split view? The answer, of course, is that we need to do some adjusting in code. We spend our lives as iPhone and iPad developers bouncing back and forth between Xcode and Interface Builder. Let's head back to Xcode and change what happens at launch time.

2.2 Connecting to the Split View Controller

Why has nothing changed? You'll find the answer in the method application:didFinishLaunchingWithOptions:.[2]

---

2. We've modified the template to call self.window instead of window and to call self.navigationController instead of navigationController so that we're using the accessor methods instead of directly addressing the ivars.

SplitVC/DailyShoot3/Classes/DailyShootAppDelegate.m

```
- (BOOL)application:(UIApplication *)application
didFinishLaunchingWithOptions:(NSDictionary *)launchOptions {
    [self.window addSubview:self.navigationController.view];
    [self.window makeKeyAndVisible];
    return YES;
}
```

Even though we've now set up a split view in IB, we are still adding the navigation controller's view as our main view. To fix that, we're going to need to add an outlet for the split view controller, which we'll name splitVC. Add this outlet to the app delegate. From this point on, we're going to assume you know that this entails the following steps:

1. In DailyShootAppDelegate.h, declare a property of type UISplitView-Controller named splitVC with the attributes nonatomic and retain, and declare the property to be an IBOutlet.[3] Save.

2. In IB, use the Connections inspector to connect this new outlet to the UISplitViewController instance. Save.

3. Synthesize the new property in DailyShootAppDelegate.m.

4. Clean up your memory by adding [splitVC release], splitVC=nil; to the dealloc method.

Remember that you can always check your work against the current stage of the code we're building. In this case, you can look in the code download at the project in the DailyShoot4 directory.

Apple recommends you use the following check to determine whether your code is running on the iPad or the iPhone:

```
UI_USER_INTERFACE_IDIOM() == UIUserInterfaceIdiomPad
```

In our case, we'll use the split view controller's view as the top view if the code is running on an iPad, and we'll use the navigation controller's view if the code is running on an iPhone.

SplitVC/DailyShoot4/Classes/DailyShootAppDelegate.m

```
- (BOOL)application:(UIApplication *)application
            didFinishLaunchingWithOptions:(NSDictionary *)launchOptions {
    if (UI_USER_INTERFACE_IDIOM() == UIUserInterfaceIdiomPad) {
        [self.window addSubview:self.splitVC.view];
```

---

3. We're assuming you're running the most recent simulator and no longer have to declare the corresponding ivar. Also remember that this variable is really a pointer to an instance of UISplitViewController even though we casually refer to splitVC as being a UISplit-ViewController.

```
    } else {
        [self.window addSubview:self.navigationController.view];
    }
    [self.window makeKeyAndVisible];
    return YES;
}
```

Build and run, and you'll see something like this:

It looks pretty. Try it in different orientations, and you should see the navigation portion of the page slide on and off the screen as the device rotates. If the application does not rotate as you rotate the device, check that you have implemented the method shouldAutorotateToInterfaceOrientation: to return YES both in RootViewController.m and in AssignmentViewController.m.

As often seems to be the case, there is good news and bad news. The good news is that the detail view of the split view is filled with the default Assignments page even before the user has selected a specific assignment. You can see from the viewDidLoad: method in AssignmentViewController.m that this is an accidental benefit that comes from trying to load the page http://dailyshoot.com/assignments/ with nothing following the final forward slash.

As mentioned in this chapter's introduction, we're going to need to fix some issues in landscape view and other issues in portrait view. We'll begin by making our fix for landscape view. To see what's wrong, select one of the assignments in the navigation view at the left of your screen.

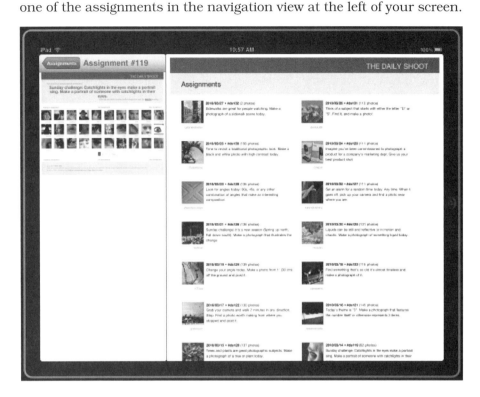

This is the behavior we expected in the iPhone version. We are pushing the detail view for the item selected in the table view on top of the table view instead of leaving the table view visible, and we are updating the web page being displayed on the right side of the screen. Let's fix this problem now.

2.3 Communicating Between the View Controllers

Let's start by building a two-way connection between the controllers that are responsible for each part of the split view. Create an outlet named rootVC of type RootViewController in the AssignmentViewController class and an outlet named assignmentVC of type AssignmentViewController in the RootViewController class.

The only nib that contains both of these objects is the MainWindow-iPad nib. Make your connections there.

We have several options for implementing the correct behavior for both platforms at once. Let's look at two variations on customizing the table view's delegate depending on the device the application is running on. First we'll modify the RootViewController so that it is the delegate for the table view on both devices. In the next section, we'll try a different approach that involves having parallel sets of view controllers for the iPhone and iPad implementations. You should understand both of these approaches, but we'll work with the second version for the rest of this chapter.

Currently the RootViewController object is the delegate for the table view. We can modify the delegate method tableView:didSelectRowAtIndexPath: like this:[4]

SplitVC/DailyShoot5/Classes/RootViewController.m

```
- (void)tableView:(UITableView *)tableView
didSelectRowAtIndexPath:(NSIndexPath *)indexPath {
▶     if (UI_USER_INTERFACE_IDIOM() == UIUserInterfaceIdiomPad) {
▶         self.assignmentVC.assignmentNumber =
▶                     [self.assignments assignmentAtIndex:indexPath.row];
▶         [self.assignmentVC loadSelectedPage];
▶     } else {
        AssignmentViewController *detailViewController =
        [[AssignmentViewController alloc]
         initWithNibName:@"AssignmentViewController" bundle:nil];
        detailViewController.assignmentNumber =
        [self.assignments assignmentAtIndex:indexPath.row];
        [self.navigationController pushViewController:detailViewController
                                        animated:YES];
        [detailViewController release];
▶     }
}
```

In other words, if the device is the iPhone, then create a new instance of AssignmentViewController, configure it, and push it on the navigation stack, as before. If instead we are running on an iPad, then use the existing instance of the AssignmentViewController, configure it, and reload the web browser using this information.

2.4 Targeting Different Devices with Subclasses

Our code is beginning to be littered with checks for what device we're on. Remember that the amount of time you will tend to spend maintain-

---

4. If you're getting compiler warnings or errors, check that you've added the @class forward declarations and imports and also declared the loadSelectedPage method.

ing code is much greater than the amount of time you spend writing it. Tracing through behavior on the iPhone or iPad becomes difficult with these if statements sprinkled here and there in a large project.

There's nothing iPad-specific in this advice. When you think that your code is filled with conditionals, use your traditional bag of tricks to split methods and classes so that the intent of the code is clearer.

For example, a more robust approach is to split your class files into three different categories. All your code that is shared between the two platforms is placed in shared files. You'll create subclasses for code that needs to be customized for the iPhone or iPad. By the end of the next section, our source code will consist of the following files:[5]

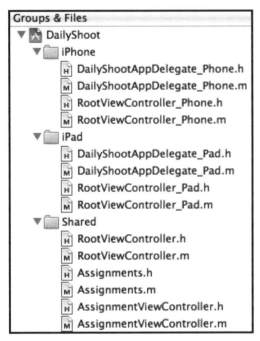

To begin with, consider the RootViewController. The only place in which we've customized its behavior to target a device is in the implementation of the table view delegate's tableView:didSelectRowAtIndexPath: method. We'll eliminate this method from the RootViewController class and create two subclasses that implement it.

Create a subclass of RootViewController named RootViewController_Pad. The header file is pretty sparse.

---

5. You can add three new groups named Shared, iPad, and iPhone and move the appropriate source files inside.

```
SplitVC/DailyShoot6/Classes/RootViewController_Pad.h
```

```objc
#import "RootViewController.h"


@interface RootViewController_Pad : RootViewController {
}
@end
```

There's not much to the implementation file either. We implement the delegate method with the iPad-specific code. You can cut and paste the appropriate lines from the tableView:didSelectRowAtIndexPath: method in RootViewController.m.

```
SplitVC/DailyShoot6/Classes/RootViewController_Pad.m
```

```objc
#import "RootViewController_Pad.h"
#import "Assignments.h"
#import "AssignmentViewController.h"


@implementation RootViewController_Pad

- (void)tableView:(UITableView *)tableView
        didSelectRowAtIndexPath:(NSIndexPath *)indexPath {
    self.assignmentVC.assignmentNumber =
    [self.assignments assignmentAtIndex:indexPath.row];
    [self.assignmentVC loadSelectedPage];
}
@end
```

We'll follow the same pattern to handle the iPhone case. Create a second subclass of RootViewController named RootViewController_Phone.

```
SplitVC/DailyShoot6/Classes/RootViewController_Phone.h
```

```objc
#import "RootViewController.h"


@interface RootViewController_Phone : RootViewController {
}
@end
```

Its implementation of the delegate method contains the iPhone-specific behavior. Again, cut and paste the appropriate lines from the table-View:didSelectRowAtIndexPath: method in RootViewController.m.

```
SplitVC/DailyShoot6/Classes/RootViewController_Phone.m
```

```objc
#import "RootViewController_Phone.h"
#import "Assignments.h"
#import "AssignmentViewController.h"


@implementation RootViewController_Phone
```

```
- (void)tableView:(UITableView *)tableView
            didSelectRowAtIndexPath:(NSIndexPath *)indexPath {
    AssignmentViewController *detailViewController =
    [[AssignmentViewController alloc]
     initWithNibName:@"AssignmentViewController" bundle:nil];
    detailViewController.assignmentNumber =
    [self.assignments assignmentAtIndex:indexPath.row];
    [self.navigationController pushViewController:detailViewController
                                    animated:YES];
    [detailViewController release];
}
@end
```

We've easily split out the device-specific behavior using subclasses of RootViewController. Delete the implementation of tableView:didSelectRow-AtIndexPath: from RootViewController.m. The superclass has all the table view's data source methods, and we've moved the device-specific delegate methods down to the subclasses.

Unfortunately, the rest of our application doesn't know anything about these new subclasses yet. Let's split the app delegate into an iPhone and an iPad-specific class and call the appropriate RootViewController subclass from each.

2.5 Separating the App Delegates

We need to make a few more changes so that the appropriate subclass of the RootViewController will be used. We're going to create separate application delegates for each platform. We'll keep the code that is common to both devices in the common superclass DailyShootAppDelegate. Here's its header file:

```
SplitVC/DailyShoot6/Classes/DailyShootAppDelegate.h
```

```
#import <UIKit/UIKit.h>

@interface DailyShootAppDelegate : NSObject <UIApplicationDelegate> {
}
@property (nonatomic, retain) IBOutlet UIWindow *window;
@property (nonatomic, retain) IBOutlet UINavigationController *navigationController;

@end
```

The implementation file removes the check for the target device. We'll defer adding the initial view to the subclasses.

Here's DailyShootAppDelegate.m:

SplitVC/DailyShoot6/Classes/DailyShootAppDelegate.m

```
#import "DailyShootAppDelegate.h"

@implementation DailyShootAppDelegate

@synthesize window, navigationController;

- (BOOL)application:(UIApplication *)application
        didFinishLaunchingWithOptions:(NSDictionary *)launchOptions {
    [self.window makeKeyAndVisible];
    return YES;
}

- (void)dealloc {
        [navigationController release], navigationController = nil ;
        [window release], window = nil ;
        [super dealloc];
}

@end
```

Create a DailyShootAppDelegate_Phone class with this header:

SplitVC/DailyShoot6/Classes/DailyShootAppDelegate_Phone.h

```
#import <UIKit/UIKit.h>
#import "DailyShootAppDelegate.h"

@interface DailyShootAppDelegate_Phone :DailyShootAppDelegate  {
}
@end
```

In the case of the iPhone, we are adding the navigation controller's view as the top-level view and calling the superclass' application:didFinishLaunchingWithOptions: method.

SplitVC/DailyShoot6/Classes/DailyShootAppDelegate_Phone.m

```
#import "DailyShootAppDelegate_Phone.h"

@implementation DailyShootAppDelegate_Phone

- (BOOL)application:(UIApplication *)application
        didFinishLaunchingWithOptions:(NSDictionary *)launchOptions {
    [self.window addSubview:self.navigationController.view];
    return [super application:application
didFinishLaunchingWithOptions:launchOptions];
}

@end
```

Similarly, create a DailyShootAppDelegate_Pad class with this header:

SplitVC/DailyShoot6/Classes/DailyShootAppDelegate_Pad.h

```
#import <UIKit/UIKit.h>
#import "DailyShootAppDelegate.h"

@interface DailyShootAppDelegate_Pad :DailyShootAppDelegate  {
}
@property (nonatomic, retain) IBOutlet UISplitViewController *splitVC;
@end
```

We need to add a property for the split view controller in this subclass. In the implementation, we'll add the split view controller's view as the top-level view and clean up that object in the dealloc method.

SplitVC/DailyShoot6/Classes/DailyShootAppDelegate_Pad.m

```
#import "DailyShootAppDelegate_Pad.h"

@implementation DailyShootAppDelegate_Pad

@synthesize splitVC;

- (BOOL)application:(UIApplication *)application
        didFinishLaunchingWithOptions:(NSDictionary *)launchOptions {
    [self.window addSubview:self.splitVC.view];
    return [super application:application
didFinishLaunchingWithOptions:launchOptions];
}
- (void)dealloc {
    [splitVC release], splitVC = nil;
    [super dealloc];
}
@end
```

We're almost done. We need to make a few small adjustments to our nib files. Open the MainWindow.xib file in IB, use the Identity inspector to change the type of the DailyShootAppDelegate object to DailyShootAppDelegate_Phone, and change the type of the RootViewController object to RootViewController_Phone.

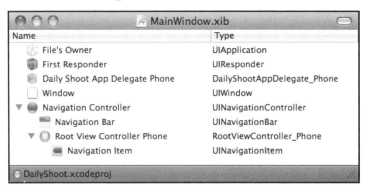

Similarly, open the MainWindow-iPad.xib file in Interface Builder, again use the Identity inspector to change the type of the DailyShootAppDelegate object to DailyShootAppDelegate_Pad, and change the type of the RootViewController object to RootViewController_Pad.

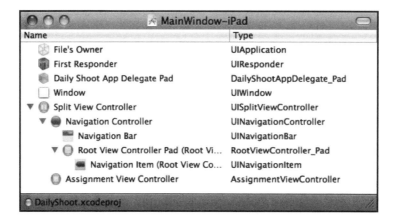

Save all of your changes, build and run, and everything should run as before.

Wow! This felt like a lot of steps to replace two simple if statements. On the other hand, your code is now more readable and flexible. You also probably found that it took very little for you to implement these changes—it just seemed like a lot to do when we spell it out explicitly on these pages.

2.6 Adding a Toolbar to the Detail View

Next, let's add a toolbar to the top of the view managed by the AssignmentViewController in the iPad version but not in the iPhone version. We're going to soon need a toolbar in the portrait orientation of the iPad version, and including it in the landscape version as well gives it a cleaner look. We already have the navigation bar in the iPhone version, so we want to make sure we don't add an additional toolbar there.

We'll create an iPad version of the AssignmentViewController class with a corresponding nib. Select the iPad group, and create a new file that is a subclass of UIViewController. Make sure you have the boxes checked to target this for iPad and to create the XIB. Name the new class AssignmentViewController_Pad.

Add a property named toolbar of type UIToolbar to the AssignmentViewController_Pad class, and mark it as an outlet. Change the superclass from the generic UIViewController to AssignmentViewController.

SplitVC/DailyShoot7/Classes/AssignmentViewController_Pad.h

```
#import "AssignmentViewController.h"


@interface AssignmentViewController_Pad : AssignmentViewController  {
}
@property(nonatomic, retain) IBOutlet UIToolbar *toolbar;
@end
```

Open the AssignmentViewController_Pad nib file. Position a UIToolbar at the top of the view, and fill the rest of it with a UIWebView. Remove the button from the toolbar. We'll create our own later. Select Scales Pages to Fit in the web view's Attributes inspector. Connect the two outlets from the File's Owner to these elements. Save.

For now, there's not much to our implementation file for the AssignmentViewController_Pad class:

SplitVC/DailyShoot7/Classes/AssignmentViewController_Pad.m

```
#import "AssignmentViewController_Pad.h"

@implementation AssignmentViewController_Pad
@synthesize toolbar;

- (BOOL)shouldAutorotateToInterfaceOrientation:
            (UIInterfaceOrientation)interfaceOrientation {
    return YES;
}
- (void)dealloc {
    [toolbar release], toolbar = nil;
    [super dealloc];
}
@end
```

As before, we need to make some adjustments to the MainWindow-iPad nib. Use the Identity inspector to change the type of the AssignmentViewController object to AssignmentViewController_Pad. You will also have to use the Attributes inspector to change the NIB name to AssignmentViewController_Pad.

Build and run to see the newly added toolbar. Next we'll use this toolbar as we work with the split view and a new iPad widget called a popover.

2.7 The Split View Delegate

Our application now looks and works great—at least in landscape.

Look what happens when we turn it on its side. The navigation disappears, and we have no easy way to navigate to one of the first 125 assignments.

Fortunately, Apple provides us with a mechanism for giving our users this ability, and Apple makes it very easy to implement.

When the user holds the iPad in landscape orientation, we want the application to appear just as it does right now. When the user switches to portrait, we will add an Assignments button to the toolbar. When the user presses the button, they will get a list of the assignments, and they will be able to select one as before. Once they've selected a specific assignment (or if they change their mind and decide not to choose one), we'll need to clear the list away.

The split view controller manages two subcontrollers. In our case, when the iPad is rotated, the split view controller either hides or reveals the view controlled by the RootViewController_Pad instance and repositions and resizes the view controlled by the AssignmentViewController_Pad object. The view managed by the AssignmentViewController_Pad is the one that will be changing during this repositioning. This means that the AssignmentViewController_Pad object will be the delegate for the UISplitViewController.

Add the declaration for the UISplitViewControllerDelegate protocol to the AssignmentViewController_Pad.h header file. Now wire up this delegate. Open the MainWindow-iPad nib, and connect the UISplitViewController's delegate outlet to the AssignmentViewController_Pad object.

Two of the methods in the UISplitViewControllerDelegate protocol will be called by the system as the device switches orientations. Much of the work you need to accomplish is taken care of for you. In fact, the names of the methods that you'll meet in the next two sections are longer than their implementations! We'll start with the one that is called when we orient the iPad vertically.

2.8 Adding a Popover

The iPad has a new widget called a *popover*, which is, of course, managed by a popover controller. It's something like a menu, but it is not attached to the button you press to make it appear. As you'll see in Chapter 4, *Popovers and Modal Dialog Boxes*, you can set popovers to appear when the user touches some specific area of the screen. For now, we'll bring up our popover when a button is pressed.

We're going to implement a method in the UISplitViewControllerDelegate protocol to add a button to the toolbar, which, when pressed, will bring up a popover containing all the items from the navigation view.

Add a property named popoverController of type UIPopoverController to AssignmentViewController_Pad.h. We don't actually need this variable in the step where we are adding the popover controller, but we will need it in the next section when we ensure that we remove the popover.

Go to the docs for the UISplitViewControllerDelegate, and copy and paste the signature for this method:

```
- (void)splitViewController:(UISplitViewController*)svc
     willHideViewController:(UIViewController *)aViewController
         withBarButtonItem:(UIBarButtonItem*)barButtonItem
       forPopoverController:(UIPopoverController*)pc
```

Yes, copy and paste. This is a delegate method, and if you make even the smallest of typos, the method will not get called at runtime, and you will get no error or warning to tell you why.

This method is called when the user switches from landscape to portrait and the RootViewController_Pad's view is about to be hidden. Notice that this method passes handles to that view controller as its second parameter and to the button on the toolbar as its third parameter. The method's last parameter is a popover controller.

To implement the method, set the title for the button, display the button on the toolbar, and set the value of the popoverController property.

SplitVC/DailyShoot8/Classes/AssignmentViewController_Pad.m

```
- (void)splitViewController:(UISplitViewController*)svc
     willHideViewController:(UIViewController *)aViewController
         withBarButtonItem:(UIBarButtonItem*)barButtonItem
       forPopoverController:(UIPopoverController*)pc {
    barButtonItem.title = aViewController.title;
    [self.toolbar setItems:[NSArray arrayWithObject:barButtonItem]
                animated:YES];
    self.popoverController = pc;
}
```

That's it. Try it. The button and the popover should appear fine in portrait. Things aren't quite right in landscape, but we'll fix that in a minute.

Hang on a minute. How did the popover get filled with the assignments that used to be listed in RootViewController? It's one of those bits of magic that should just make you smile. When the delegate method is called, the view controller that is being hidden—in our case the RootViewController—is one of the parameters, and the popover controller that we want to fill with its information is another parameter. That's how your popover is populated with the contents of the view that is being hidden when the iPad is rotated. Pretty cool.

2.9 Removing the Popover and the Button

Now that you've taken our app for a test-drive, you probably noticed a couple of details that need to be taken care of. First, if you select an assignment from the list on the popover, the new page loads behind the popover, but the popover itself doesn't go away. Let's change this so that any time the page loads, we dismiss the popover.

SplitVC/DailyShoot8/Classes/AssignmentViewController_Pad.m

```objc
- (void) loadSelectedPage {
    [super loadSelectedPage];
    if (self.popoverController) {
        [self.popoverController dismissPopoverAnimated:YES];
    }
}
```

Second, you may have noticed that when you switch the app back to landscape, the button remains in the toolbar. To fix this, just implement the following delegate method for the split view controller:

SplitVC/DailyShoot8/Classes/AssignmentViewController_Pad.m

```objc
- (void)splitViewController: (UISplitViewController*)svc
      willShowViewController:(UIViewController *)aViewController
   invalidatingBarButtonItem:(UIBarButtonItem *)barButtonItem {
    [self.toolbar setItems:[NSArray array] animated:YES];
    self.popoverController = nil;
}
```

Congratulations. You now have a universal application that works like a native navigation-based app on your iPhone and like a split view–based app on your iPad.

2.10 Creating an iPad-Only, Split View–Based App

As an exercise, now that we have a universal app that works on both platforms, start over and create an iPad-only app. Create a new Xcode project using the Split View-based Application template. You should find that you are able to use fewer nibs and classes than we did in this running example.

Try this yourself; here is a quick sketch of how you might implement one possible solution with as few changes to the code created by the template as possible.

Create a new split view–based app named DailyShoot-iPad. Bring in the source files for the Assignments class. Add an outlet for an object of type Assignments named assignments to the RootViewController class. Add an object of type Assignments to the MainWindow nib, and connect the outlet.

Modify the data source methods in the RootViewController to return the values from the assignments property.

The DetailViewController is taking the place of our AssignmentViewController. Replace its UILabel with the UIWebView; we need to do this both in the DetailView nib file and in the controller's source code files.

We'll use the template's detailItem to hold our assignment number. We can change its type to NSNumber. Back in RootViewController.m, implement the table view delegate method like this:

SplitVC/DailyShootiPad/Classes/RootViewController.m

```
- (void)tableView:(UITableView *)aTableView
        didSelectRowAtIndexPath:(NSIndexPath *)indexPath {
    self.detailViewController.detailItem =
                    [self.assignments assignmentAtIndex:indexPath.row];
}
```

All that remains is to implement the configureView method in DetailViewController.m to display the selected web page and the viewDidLoad view to display the list of all assignments at launch.

SplitVC/DailyShootiPad/Classes/DetailViewController.m

```
- (void)configureView {
    NSString *url =
    [NSString stringWithFormat:@"http://dailyshoot.com/assignments/%@",
     self.detailItem];
    [self.webView loadRequest:
     [NSURLRequest requestWithURL:[NSURL URLWithString:url]]];
}
-(void)viewDidLoad {
    [super viewDidLoad];
    [self configureView];
}
```

You should also change the text on the toolbar button in DetailViewController.m and change the title text for the RootViewController to read Assignments. Add your custom icons and launch screen.

You can view this solution to the exercise in the code download in the SplitVC/DailyShootiPad directory.

2.11 Summary

As with most Cocoa and iPhone development, we've accomplished a lot in this chapter without writing a lot of code. We've added a split view and its controller to our project, and we've enabled communication between the two subviews through their controllers. These were the same controllers, the RootViewController and the AssignmentViewController, that we used in the previous chapter.

With very little modification, we transformed this from an iPhone app running on an iPad to an app with a native iPad look and feel. We learned how to test which device the app is running on and coded it so the behavior was correct on each device. We learned how to respond to which orientation the device is running in and how best to support each orientation. We saw how easy it was to implement a popover that was filled with the same content as the hidden navigation view.

For the remainder of the book, we are going to build iPad-only applications. We are going to work with the new APIs and techniques that are designed to take advantage of the additional size provided by this new device. At this point, you should feel free to read the book in any order you like. Jump right into gestures, or head over to movies. If you want to learn more about popovers, you may want to start with Chapter 4, *Popovers and Modal Dialog Boxes*, on page 75.

Chapter 3

Using Gestures

The iPad's large surface isn't just for viewing; it's for getting your hands in the mix and using gestures to interact with your applications. Of course, the iPhone also uses Multi-Touch as its primary means of interaction, but its small screen constrains us from fully exploring gestures and ultimately limits our ability to create an immersive experience.

There's another aspect of the iPhone that made using gestures in your applications challenging—the SDK. To write gestures, you had to copy and paste Multi-Touch code between classes and applications, without any convenient means for reuse. Beginning in iOS 3.2, Apple has refined the way gestures fit into the UIKit architecture and given you the ability to abstract and reuse gestures on the iPad (and as of iOS 4.0, you have the same tools available to you on the iPhone). Apple has also provided some ready-made gestures for you to use, including taps, pans, pinches, rotation, and swipes—and, if the built-in gestures don't meet your needs, you can easily extend the new architecture and write your own.

As you'll see in this chapter, Apple has significantly improved the tools at hand to create gestures, but keep in mind there is a fair bit to know when using prebuilt recognizers (or writing new gesture recognizers), and in this chapter we'll explore the gestures in detail; we'll start by using and configuring prebuilt recognizers and then add more sophisticated behavior, customizing and controlling how the recognizers behave. Finally, we'll create a recognizer to look for our own custom gesture. Let's get started!

3.1 iPad Virtual Bubble Wrap

Who would have thought when the Sealed Air Corporation invented BubbleWrap™ in 1957 that it would take on a life of its own as an addictive and satisfying activity for all ages?[1] After all, when presented with a fresh sheet of all those air-filled bubbles, who doesn't want to start popping them?

Of course, another invention, the Internet, came along and brought with it *virtual* bubble wrap; and today, all you have to say is "bubble wrap" to hear the response "There's an App for That!" Bubble wrap has found its way onto the iPhone. What's next? Virtual bubble wrap for the iPad, of course—just imagine all that screen space and Multi-Touch gestures devoted to popping simulated, air-filled bubbles.

In this chapter, we're going to create our own virtual bubble wrap application and fully explore the new gesture APIs in the process. Rather than present a conventional sheet of bubbles that can be popped, we're going to use gestures to make things a little more interesting. In this application, you will create your own custom bubble wrap layouts (through tap gestures), pop all the bubbles you want (using the tap gesture in a slightly different manner), resize bubbles (with a pinch gesture), swipe the screen and start over (through a swipe gesture), and even implement a custom gesture that will allow you to delete bubbles.

To get started, we're going to do the following:

1. Create a simple view-based application to act as a "bubble sheet."

2. Use a built-in gesture to capture a "tap" and place a bubble on the sheet for each tap.

3. Reuse this tap gesture to pop the bubble.

Once we have the basics, we'll circle back and add resizing, swiping, and deletion—all through gestures.

---

1. If you aren't familiar with BubbleWrap, it is a transparent sheet of plastic embedded with air-filled bubbles that is used as a protective means of packaging items for shipping. Many hours of entertainment have resulted from squeezing the air bubbles (and producing the loud pop that accompanies it).

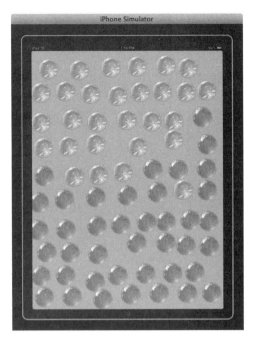

Figure 3.1: THE BUBBLE WRAP INTERFACE

3.2 Using Simple Tap Gestures

Before we dive in, we have time for a quick pep talk; if you have experience with the UIKit views and you have even a passing familiarity of Multi-Touch events, then understanding the new gesture design is straightforward. The new architecture revolves around gesture recognizers you can instantiate and attach to any view. These recognizers act as observers of Multi-Touch events and get a peek at them before your views do. Recognizers process Multi-Touch events until their gesture is recognized and then send an action message to a target that you specify; if your recognizer doesn't find a gesture in a sequence of Multi-Touch events, the events are passed on to other recognizers (if you have any) and, ultimately, if no gesture is recognized, to the view itself. With that short summary out of the way, the best way to understand gestures is to see them in action, so let's get the implementation started.

To get this thing rolling, we've already created a project named Bubbles1, which you'll find in the gestures folder in the sample code; to give the application more of a bubble wrap feel, we've taken the liberty of opening the Bubbles1ViewController.xib nib file in Interface Builder and changing the background of the main view to a nice medium gray. For dramatic effect (that you'll see later), we also changed the main window's background color to solid black in the MainWindow.xib nib file. Finally, we've placed two images in the project, one of an inflated bubble (named bubble.png) and one of a popped bubble (named popped.png).

Instantiating the Gesture

Our first coding task is to create a tap gesture that, when recognized, will result in a bubble being placed on the main application view. To accomplish that, we override viewDidLoad in the Bubbles1ViewController and instantiate a tap recognizer. Let's take a look:

gestures/Bubbles1/Classes/Bubbles1ViewController.m

```
- (void)viewDidLoad {
        [super viewDidLoad];

        UITapGestureRecognizer *tapRecognizer =
                [[UITapGestureRecognizer alloc]
                 initWithTarget:self
                 action:@selector(handleTapFrom:)];
}
```

Here we instantiate a tap recognizer by calling UITapGestureRecognizer's initWithTarget:action: method. Gesture recognizers use the common Cocoa target-action pattern, whereby a target will be sent an action message when the gesture is recognized. We've designated self as the target and handleTapFrom: as the action, so when this gesture is recognized, the handleTapFrom method will be called on our instance of Bubbles1ViewController.

Attaching the Gesture to a View

With any gesture, after you instantiate it, you're going to need to configure it through its properties, and you're going to have to attach it to a view for it to be useful. Here's how we do that with our tap recognizer:

gestures/Bubbles1/Classes/Bubbles1ViewController.m

```
- (void)viewDidLoad {
        [super viewDidLoad];

        UITapGestureRecognizer *tapRecognizer =
                [[UITapGestureRecognizer alloc]
                 initWithTarget:self
                 action:@selector(handleTapFrom:)];
        [tapRecognizer setNumberOfTapsRequired:1];
```

```
▶        [self.view addGestureRecognizer:tapRecognizer];
▶        [tapRecognizer release];
}
```

We first configure the recognizer through its setNumberOfTapsRequired: method, allowing us to specify how many taps the recognizer should look for. In this case, one tap is probably going to be the most natural gesture for our users. As you can probably guess, the setNumberOfTaps-Required: method is specific to a tap recognizer; we are going to see that other types of recognizers have their own specific configuration properties.

We then take the Bubbles1ViewController's view and attach the tapRecognizer using the addGestureRecognizer method—a new method added to UIView's interface in iOS 3.2. Once the recognizer is attached to a view, it gets to observe all Multi-Touch events that hit the view to look for gestures.

Finally, as good citizens, we release the recognizer now that the view owns it.

Acting on the Gesture

Now that we have the tap recognizer instantiated and attached to a view, we need to implement the specific behavior for the action—placing a bubble on the view. How do we approach that? We're going to need to determine the location of the tap, and then we'll need to create an image representing the bubble and add it to the Bubbles1ViewController's view. So, let's write a handleTapFrom: method that determines the location of the tap and creates a bubble:

`gestures/Bubbles1/Classes/Bubbles1ViewController.m`

```
- (void)handleTapFrom:(UITapGestureRecognizer *)recognizer {
        CGPoint location = [recognizer locationInView:self.view];

        CGRect rect = CGRectMake(location.x - 40,
                location.y - 40, 80.0f, 80.0f);
        UIImageView *image = [[UIImageView alloc]
                initWithFrame:rect];
        [image setImage:[UIImage imageNamed:@"bubble.png"]];

        [self.view addSubview:image];

        [image release];
}
```

Let's step through this code: handleTapFrom: is passed the recognizer object that accepted the gesture.[2] We can use the recognizer to determine the location where the tap occurred by using its locationInView: method, which, given a view, will tell us the point within that view where the gesture occurred. Here we're most interested in the location of the tap within the Bubbles1ViewController's view, so we pass self.view as the view.

Now that we have the point where the tap occurred, we need to create a bubble and place it at that location. We do that by computing a bounding box for the image (using the tap location as a guide), instantiating an image with that bounding box, and setting the source of the image to bubbles.png. Finally, all we need to do is add the image as a subview to our self.view.

Creating Some Bubbles

At this point, you're ready to test this code. Build and run the project, and you should see a blank, gray screen—simply tap within the view (or click using the simulator), and you should see bubbles appear under your taps.

Before we go further, let's step back to think about what we've done:

- We created a tap gesture recognizer and configured it to recognize a one-tap gesture.

- We attached that gesture object to our Bubbles1ViewController's view, so any time Multi-Touch events occur on that view, our gesture recognizer gets a peek at those events and can decide whether they constitute a tap.

- And, assuming there is a tap, we told the gesture recognizer to call the handleTapFrom: method on our Bubbles1ViewController.

- We also wrote the code for the handleTapFrom: method, which determines the location of the tap from the recognizer object and then creates an image that looks like a bubble and places it at that location.

Not bad for such a small amount of code, huh? Now let's make things more interesting by enhancing the bubbles so they can be popped.

---

2. We'll discuss precisely what it means to accept a gesture later in the chapter; for now, when a tap recognizer sees a Multi-Touch set of events that look like a tap gesture, it recognizes the gesture and invokes the action on the target.

3.3   Multi-Touch Events and the View Hierarchy

To create a popped-bubble effect, we need to know when a user taps a bubble. How do we accomplish that? You might be thinking that one way of recognizing when a bubble (or in our case a UIImageView representing a bubble) is tapped is to attach another tap gesture to each UIImageView and write another action to handle the rest. That would work, and in fact we're going to implement a resize gesture by attaching a gesture directly to an image view, but here we're going to take another, more direct path to demonstrate how the view hierarchy works with touches. The next several paragraphs are important because they go into the detail of how Multi-Touch events work with the view hierarchy and how they relate to gestures. Let's work through the details and then get these bubbles working.

When the iPad receives a Multi-Touch event, by default it passes the touch from the application to the window to the window's view and down recursively into each subview for which the touch falls within its bounds. The final view in the hierarchy, for which the touch falls within, is called the *hit-tested* view. When it comes to recognizing gestures, the hit-tested view gets the first shot at recognizing Multi-Touch events and, if they aren't recognized, passes them up the chain to the parent views (or ultimately on to the window and application, if no view makes use of them).

In our current code, when a user touches the UIImageView of a bubble, that view gets first crack at recognizing the touch as a gesture; and if it isn't recognized, the events go to the parent view, which is our Bubbles1ViewController's view. Because we haven't added a gesture or any code to recognize Multi-Touch events in the UIImageView, the events will always go to the Bubbles1ViewController's view, and taps will be recognized there, even if we're tapping one of the bubble images.

This all sounds a bit complicated; why not just install another gesture on the UIImageView and be done with it? Well, using the knowledge of the view hierarchy and hit testing, we can write much simpler code to implement bubble popping, and in general, you'll be able to use gestures in a more sophisticated way with your new understanding of Multi-Touch events (in fact, we'll make direct use of this writing our own custom gesture later in the chapter).

Implementing the Bubble Pop

Now that you have some background, it's time to use your new knowledge. Here's how we're going to approach writing the code to pop a bubble: we're going to use the existing tap gesture we've already attached to the Bubbles1ViewController's view. When a user taps a bubble, the touch event will first hit the bubble's UIImageView, which has no gesture to deal with it—so it will propagate to the Bubbles1ViewController's view, where our current gesture will recognize the tap. At that point, when the handleTapFrom: method is called, we're going to determine (using hit testing) which view was tapped, and if it was one of our UIImageViews, we're going to change its source image to popped.png, as we've depicted here:

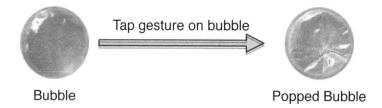

Bubble   Popped Bubble

Let's take a look at the code; you'll find the handleTapFrom: action with some new additions:

gestures/Bubbles2/Classes/Bubbles2ViewController.m

```
- (void)handleTapFrom:(UITapGestureRecognizer *)recognizer {
        CGPoint location = [recognizer locationInView:self.view];

        UIView *hitView = [self.view hitTest:location withEvent:nil];
        if ([hitView isKindOfClass:[UIImageView class]]) {

                [(UIImageView *)hitView
                        setImage:[UIImage imageNamed:@"popped.png"]];

        } else {
                CGRect rect = CGRectMake(location.x - 40,
                        location.y - 40, 80.0f, 80.0f);
                UIImageView *image =
                        [[UIImageView alloc] initWithFrame:rect];
                [image setImage:[UIImage imageNamed:@"bubble.png"]];
                [image setUserInteractionEnabled: YES];

                [self.view addSubview:image];

                [image release];
        }
}
```

Recall from your previous version of this method that you first obtain the location of the tap from the recognizer. Our new code takes this location and calls hitTest:withEvent: to obtain the hit-tested view. If this tap is on a bubble, it will be on a UIImageView, and if not, it will be on the Bubbles1ViewController's view.

Given that, all we need to do is test whether the hit-tested view is an UIImageView and, if so, to change the image from bubbles.png to popped.png. On the other hand, if the hit-tested view isn't an image view, it must be our Bubbles1ViewController view, which means the user wants to place another bubble on the view. In that case, we use the same code we previously wrote.

Notice that we've made one addition to the old code to handle an issue with UIImageViews. As it turns out, image views are configured to disregard Multi-Touch events by default, so setting setUserInteractionEnabled to YES allows us to interact with image views using touch events. If we didn't set setUserInteractionEnabled to YES, we'd get the Multi-Touch event in the controller's view, but the image itself would never be a hit-tested view (and we'd never be able to pop bubbles).

Testing the Bubble Wrap

You're now ready to build and run the fully functional bubble wrap. Try tapping the blank areas of the view to create new bubbles and clicking bubbles to pop them. Other than perhaps adding a popping sound, which we'll leave to you to work in, we think this implementation makes for some nice virtual bubble wrap (and using very little code!).

3.4 UIGestureRecognizer and the Swipe Gesture

As mentioned, there are gestures beyond the tap gesture. In fact the UITapGestureRecognizer is part of a family of recognizers that are all subclasses of UIGestureRecognizer, an abstract class that defines the base set of functionality and interfaces for gesture recognizers. We'll get into the details of this abstract class a little later in the chapter; for now, we're going to look at another of its subclasses: UISwipeGestureRecognizer.

Recognizing a Swipe

We're going to use the swipe gesture to clear the bubble sheet to give us a nice clean surface to create new bubbles. In other words, when you use a finger to swipe across the screen, all the bubbles will be deleted, leaving you with a fresh sheet. Writing the code to recognize a swipe is similar to our tap recognizer code, with a couple items specific to the swipe gesture. Let's start by instantiating and configuring the swipe recognizer:

gestures/Bubbles3/Classes/Bubbles3ViewController.m

```
- (void)viewDidLoad {
        [super viewDidLoad];

        // our previous code goes here

▶       UISwipeGestureRecognizer *swipeRecognizer =
▶               [[UISwipeGestureRecognizer alloc]
▶                       initWithTarget:self
▶                       action:@selector(handleSwipeFrom:)];
▶       swipeRecognizer.direction = UISwipeGestureRecognizerDirectionRight |
▶               UISwipeGestureRecognizerDirectionLeft;
▶       [self.view addGestureRecognizer:swipeRecognizer];
▶       [swipeRecognizer release];
}
```

Look somewhat familiar? Let's step through the code: first, we're allocating and initializing the UISwipeGestureRecognizer class with a target and action, just like we did with the tap recognizer. In this case, we're going to write an action named handleSwipeFrom: to handle the swipe when it is recognized.

We then specify the swipe direction—there are four of them to choose from:

- UISwipeGestureRecognizerDirectionLeft

- UISwipeGestureRecognizerDirectionRight

- UISwipeGestureRecognizerDirectionUp

- UISwipeGestureRecognizerDirectionDown

We specified two directions (left and right), which need to be bitwise OR'd together, but feel free to use whatever combinations of directions you want.

After configuring the swipe recognizer, we've added the recognizer to the controller's view, just as we did with the tap recognizer. Now, we need to write the handleSwipeFrom action to take care of clearing the bubble sheet.

Clearing the Bubble Sheet

Mechanically clearing the bubble sheet is a straightforward task; all we have to do is locate the Bubbles1ViewController's subviews and remove them. If you haven't worked with subviews before, the UIViews's subviews: method returns an array of subviews, which we simply iterate over, calling removeFromSuperview: on each one. The removeFromSuperview: method removes the view from its parent view (in this case the Bubbles1ViewController view). Let's put this to work:

gestures/Bubbles3/Classes/Bubbles3ViewController.m

```
- (void)handleSwipeFrom:(UISwipeGestureRecognizer *)recognizer {
        for (UIView *subview in [self.view subviews]) {
                [subview removeFromSuperview];
        }

        [UIView beginAnimations:nil context:nil];
        [UIView setAnimationDuration:.75];
        [UIView setAnimationBeginsFromCurrentState:YES];
        [UIView
                setAnimationTransition:UIViewAnimationTransitionFlipFromLeft
                forView:self.view
                cache:YES];
        [UIView commitAnimations];
}
```

We've also decided to use a little animation to indicate that something has happened as a result of the swipe gesture. Although the point of this chapter isn't to explain the details of animation, here we're simply setting up a flip animation to happen over a duration of .75 seconds, and in this case we're just flipping the same view around, so once the image subviews are deleted, the animation should show a blank view flipping around. You'll find more on creating animations in the book we recommended earlier in the chapter, *Core Animation for Mac OS X and the iPhone: Creating Compelling Dynamic User Interfaces* [Dud08].

That's it for adding the swipe—go ahead and compile. Swipe one finger left or right across your interface, and watch a new bubble sheet flip around, ready for more bubble fun (see Figure 3.2, on the next page).

Using Multiple Fingers

The UISwipeGestureRecognizer class also has a numberOfTouchesRequired property, which can be set to the number of touches (or fingers) that must be present in the swipe gesture.

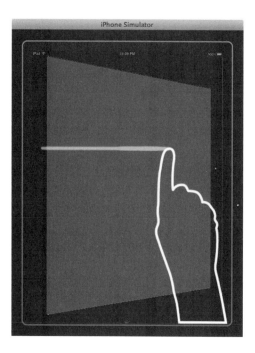

Figure 3.2: AN ANIMATED SWIPE GESTURE

For instance, if you set this property to 2, then the swipe recognizer will recognize the gesture only if two fingers are used in the swipe.[3]

The UITapGestureRecognizer also has a numberOfTouchesRequired property. Although it's less common than a multifinger swipe, you can create tap recognizers that require multiple touches, as well.

3.5 Discrete and Continuous Gestures

We've looked at two gesture recognizers so far: tap and swipe. Both send a single action message to the target when their gesture is recognized—we call these *discrete* gestures.

There's another type of recognizer that sends multiple action messages based on a single gesture, called *continuous* gestures. As an example,

---

3. Note that if you set this value greater than one, then your gestures must be tested on the actual device, because the simulator provides no way to simulate more than one finger touch (we'll see there is a way to test pinch gestures, however, in a bit).

Figure 3.3: RESIZED UIIMAGES IN THE BUBBLE WRAP APPLICATION

think about pinching an image on your iPhone (or iPad). The gesture happens over time as you pinch the image larger and smaller and continues until you lift your fingers.

Resizing Bubbles with a Pinch Gesture

Let's create a pinch gesture that allows us to resize bubbles (either larger or smaller)—you can see what that looks like in Figure 3.3. To enable the bubbles to be resized, we attach a pinch gesture directly to each UIImageView—we discussed how this could work with tap gestures on the bubble images, and now we're going to try it for real with the pinch gesture.

Rather than instantiate the pinch gesture in the viewDidLoad method, we're going to put our code in the handleTapFrom: method. If you think about it, the bubble images are created in the handleTapFrom: method, so that's the natural place to attach a gesture to them.

Let's look at the code to create the UIPinchGestureRecognizer objects:

gestures/Bubbles4/Classes/Bubbles4ViewController.m

```
- (void)handleTapFrom:(UITapGestureRecognizer *)recognizer {
        CGPoint location = [recognizer locationInView:self.view];

        UIView *hitView = [self.view hitTest:location withEvent:nil];
        if ([hitView isKindOfClass:[UIImageView class]]) {

                [(UIImageView *)hitView
                  setImage:[UIImage imageNamed:@"popped.png"]];

        } else {
                CGRect rect =
                        CGRectMake(location.x - 40,
                                location.y - 40, 80.0f, 80.0f);
                UIImageView *image =
                [[UIImageView alloc] initWithFrame:rect];
                [image setImage:[UIImage imageNamed:@"bubble.png"]];
                [image setUserInteractionEnabled: YES];

                UIPinchGestureRecognizer *pinchRecognizer =
                [[UIPinchGestureRecognizer alloc]
                 initWithTarget:self
                 action:@selector(handlePinchFrom:)];
                [image addGestureRecognizer:pinchRecognizer];
                [pinchRecognizer release];

                [self.view addSubview:image];
                [image release];
        }

}
```

This new code should look familiar; we're instantiating the UIPinchGestureRecognizer, setting its action to handlePinchFrom:, and adding the gesture to each image view. We're using this recognizer as is, without any special configuration.

With the gesture attached to a view, we can now concentrate on the more interesting task of writing the code that handles action messages from the pinch recognizer and adjusts the on-screen size of the bubble image in proportion to the amount of the pinch. To do this, we use a property of the UIPinchGestureRecognizer called scale, which represents the scale factor of the pinch.

Here's how it works: after the pinch gesture begins, the scale factor is adjusted as you pinch in and out and passed on to your action method continuously. Once you have the scale factor, all you need to do is adjust the size of the bubble image by that scale factor. Let's take a look at how you do that:

gestures/Bubbles4/Classes/Bubbles4ViewController.m
```
- (void)handlePinchFrom:(UIPinchGestureRecognizer *)recognizer {
        CGFloat scale = [recognizer scale];
        CGAffineTransform transform =
                CGAffineTransformMakeScale(scale, scale);
        recognizer.view.transform = transform;
}
```

First, we use the recognizer and retrieve its scale property, which holds a value representing the amount of scale that is indicated from the pinch gesture. Then, we use scale to create a transformation matrix. If you aren't familiar with transforms, they can be used to manipulate the coordinates of a view, giving you a natural way to scale and rotate your views—by setting the transform property of a view to a transform matrix, the view will be drawn according to how it is scaled in the matrix. Here we are assigning the transform to the view associated with the recognizer, which is one of our image views. After assigning the transform, the view will be redrawn and scaled by the values in the matrix. Transforms are a big topic outside of the scope of this book, and you can find out more in *Core Animation for Mac OS X and the iPhone: Creating Compelling Dynamic User Interfaces* [Dud08].

Testing the Pinch

That's all the code we'll need; build and run the new code. Create a few bubbles; next, touch both fingers within any bubble and then pull your fingers apart—you'll see the bubble grow in size as you do. Likewise, you can squeeze your fingers back together and shrink the bubble. If you're using the simulator, you can simulate a pinch by holding down the Option key (you should see two dots appear that represent your fingers), positioning the dots by moving your mouse (or trackpad) and then clicking and moving the mouse to simulate your fingers pinching in and out.

3.6 Creating Custom Gestures

Apple has supplied some great built-in gestures, but what do you do if they don't meet your needs? You can create your own, of course. Apple has made the process straightforward by allowing you to subclass the gesture recognizer base class to create your own gestures. That said,

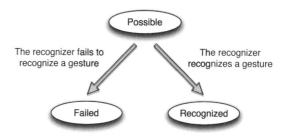

Figure 3.4: The states of a discrete gesture recognizer

writing your own recognizers does require that you have a bit more knowledge about the way gestures operate, and we'll be covering that in this section. We're also going to use this knowledge to write a custom gesture for our bubble wrap application.

How Gesture Recognizers Really Work

Think of gesture recognizers as simple state machines that transition between states based on the touch events they receive while the user interacts with the screen. All recognizers start in the same state: the UIGestureRecognizerStatePossible state, which indicates that the recognizer is examining touch events to find a gesture. Once a gesture is recognized, the discrete gestures transition to the UIGestureRecognizerStateRecognized state. If, on the other hand, the recognizer fails to find a gesture, it reaches the UIGestureRecognizerStateFailed state.

Continuous gestures handle things a little differently; like discrete gestures, they start in the UIGestureRecognizerStatePossible state, but when a continuous gesture is first recognized, the recognizer moves to the UIGestureRecognizerStateBegan. Then as the gesture changes over time, the recognizer changes the state to UIGestureRecognizerStateChanged. In fact, as the gesture continues to change, the recognizer will keep setting its state to UIGestureRecognizerStateChanged. From the changed state, continuous recognizers follow two paths: either the user lifts her fingers and the gesture moves into the UIGestureRecognizerStateEnded state or the recognizer can decide the gesture no longer is being satisfied and may switch to the UIGestureRecognizerStateCancelled state.

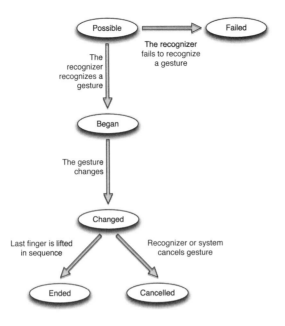

Figure 3.5: THE STATES OF A CONTINUOUS GESTURE RECOGNIZER

Let's think about these different types of recognizers in context: take a discrete recognizer, such as the single-tap recognizer. This recognizer begins life in the UIGestureRecognizerStatePossible state, and then as soon as a touch event arrives that is a tap, it simply moves to the UIGestureRecognizerStateRecognized state. On the other hand, picture a continuous recognizer for the pinch gesture. Here the recognizer enters the UIGestureRecognizerStateBegan state when two fingers are placed on the surface, and then as the fingers perform the pinch over time, the recognizer repeatedly sets the UIGestureRecognizerStateChanged state. Once the user removes her finger, the recognizer sets the UIGestureRecognizerStateEnded state.

Creating a Deletion Gesture

With that background in mind, let's talk about the gesture we're going to implement: if you were ever exposed to the Apple Newton, you might remember a gesture that required that you make a zig-zag pattern over an object, similar to the pattern you'd make with a pencil eraser. Upon recognition of that gesture, the Newton deleted the underlying object.

We're going to implement a recognizer that recognizes the same gesture, and then we'll use it to delete an underlying bubble. Think for a minute about how you'd write code to detect this gesture. Although there are many ways to analyze the Multi-Touch events to look for an eraser-like motion, we're going to see how far a simple heuristic can get us.

Here's how our heuristic works: notice that the delete gesture is really just an upward/downward motion that we can track by simply watching the motion around the y-axis. If there is a change from increasing to decreasing (or vice versa) in the y value, we know the direction of movement has changed. Further, if we count the changes, then we can, after two or three changes, decide this is a deletion gesture. Of course, this isn't perfect, and that's why we call it a *heuristic*. What could go wrong? Well, a user might make a long swipe motion that undulates a bit too much, causing the swipe look like a deletion. Or depending on the swipe algorithm (which we have no details of), perhaps a deletion gesture that is too wide might be interpreted as a swipe. How big a problem is this? It's not a big one, as you'll see, but you might find it happens now and then, given that the gestures have some similarity. That's OK; we'll fix this later in this chapter.

Subclassing the UIGestureRecognizer

It's time to get this delete recognizer written. We do this by first creating a subclass of the base recognizer; let's start by creating an interface file called DeleteGestureRecognizer.h.

```
gestures/Bubbles5/Classes/DeleteGestureRecognizer.h
#import <Foundation/Foundation.h>
#import <UIKit/UIGestureRecognizerSubclass.h>

@interface DeleteGestureRecognizer : UIGestureRecognizer {
}
@end
```

Here, we import the UIGestureRecognizerSubclass.h header file, which defines the base UIGestureRecognizer class, and declaring a new interface for DeleteGestureRecognizer, which inherits from UIGestureRecognizer.

Now we're going to add the methods that we will need to subclass from the UIGestureRecognizer. Add the following methods in your interface definition:

```
gestures/Bubbles5/Classes/DeleteGestureRecognizer.h
- (void)touchesBegan:(NSSet *)touches withEvent:(UIEvent *)event;
- (void)touchesMoved:(NSSet *)touches withEvent:(UIEvent *)event;
- (void)touchesEnded:(NSSet *)touches withEvent:(UIEvent *)event;
- (void)touchesCancelled:(NSSet *)touches withEvent:(UIEvent *)event;
- (void)reset;
```

We'll come back to each of these methods, fully describing and implementing them in the implementation file, but before we do that, we're going to add a few more additions to the interface file:

```
gestures/Bubbles5/Classes/DeleteGestureRecognizer.h
#import <Foundation/Foundation.h>
#import <UIKit/UIGestureRecognizerSubclass.h>

@interface DeleteGestureRecognizer : UIGestureRecognizer {
▶        bool strokeMovingUp;
▶        int touchChangedDirection;
▶        UIView *viewToDelete;
}

▶ @property (nonatomic, retain) UIView *viewToDelete;

- (void)touchesBegan:(NSSet *)touches withEvent:(UIEvent *)event;
- (void)touchesMoved:(NSSet *)touches withEvent:(UIEvent *)event;
- (void)touchesEnded:(NSSet *)touches withEvent:(UIEvent *)event;
- (void)touchesCancelled:(NSSet *)touches withEvent:(UIEvent *)event;
- (void)reset;

@end
```

We've added three new additions: the first is a bool variable named strokeMovingUp that is going to have the value YES if the gesture is moving in the positive y direction (and NO otherwise). Next, we add an int named touchChangedDirection that is going to hold the number of times the gestures direction is changed. Our last property is a UIView named viewToDelete that will hold a reference to the view that is going to be deleted if the gesture is recognized.

Implementing the DeleteGestureRecognizer

Now it's time to write the implementation; at this point, we'll type in the skeleton of the DeleteGestureRecognizer file:

gestures/Bubbles5/Classes/DeleteGestureRecognizer.m

```
@implementation DeleteGestureRecognizer

@synthesize viewToDelete;

@end
```

We're now going to step through each method that we're overriding from the UIGestureRecognizer class, which includes the reset method and all the methods that begin with the name *touches* in the interface file. These touch methods closely mirror the Multi-Touch event-handling framework supported by UIKit. If you're curious about how these events are handled at a level lower than gestures, check out "Handling Multi-Touch Events" in the *iPhone Application Programming Guide* [App09b]; we'll describe their role in the UIGestureRecognizer as we implement the methods in a moment.

We're going to start by implementing the reset method. This method is called to reset the recognizer any time it completes, either by recognizing a gesture or by failing; in either case, reset cleans up the mess and gets our properties ready for the next try by resetting the properties to their initial values:

gestures/Bubbles5/Classes/DeleteGestureRecognizer.m

```
- (void)reset {
        [super reset];
        strokeMovingUp = YES;
        touchChangedDirection = 0;
        self.viewToDelete = nil;
}
```

Now it's time for the various touches methods; let's take a look at them as a group to understand their function before implementing:

- The touchesBegan:withEvent: method is called when one or more fingers touch the view to which the gesture is attached.

- The touchesMoved:withEvent: method is called when those fingers begin to move.

- The touchesEnded:withEvent: method is called when one or more fingers lift up from the screen.

- The touchesCancelled:withEvent: method is called when the system decides to cancel the sequence of events (such as during an incoming phone call).

Our job is to work through each touch method, supply the right behavior, and, if necessary, change the state of the gesture. Our superclass, the UIGestureRecognizer class, will handle all the details of calling reset, sending action messages to the targets of the gesture, and doing other housekeeping details that happen behind the scenes.

Let's start with the touchesBegan:withEvent: method; this method is called when those first touches occur on the view to which your gesture is attached. The only behavior we're going to add is to make sure we call the superclass's touchesBegan:withEvent: method and that there is only one touch (that is, one finger) involved in the gesture. If there is more than one touch, we're going to immediately fail by setting the state property to UIGestureRecognizerStateFailed. That's it; it isn't too complicated so far.

gestures/Bubbles5/Classes/DeleteGestureRecognizer.m

```
- (void)touchesBegan:(NSSet *)touches withEvent:(UIEvent *)event {
        [super touchesBegan:touches withEvent:event];

        if ([touches count] != 1) {
                self.state = UIGestureRecognizerStateFailed;
                return;
        }
}
```

Our next method is touchesMoved:withEvent:, which is called whenever the gesture is moved (in other words, fingers have touched the view and then are moved by the user without lifting them). This part of the code gets more interesting.

Let's take a look:

gestures/Bubbles5/Classes/DeleteGestureRecognizer.m

```
- (void)touchesMoved:(NSSet *)touches withEvent:(UIEvent *)event {
        [super touchesMoved:touches withEvent:event];

        if (self.state == UIGestureRecognizerStateFailed) return;

        CGPoint nowPoint = [[touches anyObject] locationInView:self.view];
        CGPoint prevPoint = [[touches anyObject] previousLocationInView:self.view]

        if (strokeMovingUp == YES) {
                if (nowPoint.y < prevPoint.y ) {
                        strokeMovingUp = NO;
                        touchChangedDirection++;
                }
        } else if (nowPoint.y > prevPoint.y ) {
                strokeMovingUp = YES;
                touchChangedDirection++;
        }

}
```

As with any touch method, we need to first let the superclass have its turn. We make sure the gesture hasn't already failed, and if it has, we return. We then use the touch object to retrieve two values: the current location and the previous location of the move. With these two locations, we can easily determine whether there has been a change in direction in the gesture by comparing them.

Here, we test two cases: is the gesture moving up and then reversing course, or is the gesture moving down and then is going back up? If either is true, we change our direction indicator property strokeMovingUp and increment the number of times we've changed direction in touchChangedDirection.

Next up is the touchesEnded:withEvent: method, which is called when the user's fingers are lifted. Our job here is simple: if the touchChangedDirection property tells us we've changed direction three or more times, then we're going to recognize the gesture by setting the state property to UIGestureRecognizerStateRecognized.

If not, that leaves us only one other option: setting the state to failed.

gestures/Bubbles5/Classes/DeleteGestureRecognizer.m

```
- (void)touchesEnded:(NSSet *)touches withEvent:(UIEvent *)event {
        [super touchesEnded:touches withEvent:event];
        if (self.state == UIGestureRecognizerStatePossible) {
                if (touchChangedDirection >= 3) {
                        self.state = UIGestureRecognizerStateRecognized;
                } else {
                        self.state = UIGestureRecognizerStateFailed;
                }
        }
}
```

Finally, we have the touchesCancelled:withEvent: method, which is called when the system wants to cancel the touch events. If this happens, all we can do is set the gestures state property to UIGestureRecognizerState-Failed.

gestures/Bubbles5/Classes/DeleteGestureRecognizer.m

```
- (void)touchesCancelled:(NSSet *)touches withEvent:(UIEvent *)event {
        [super touchesCancelled:touches withEvent:event];
        [self reset];
        self.state = UIGestureRecognizerStateFailed;
}
```

Congrats! You've just written a full-fledged gesture recognizer for the iPad. Take a second to admire what you've done, and then let's get this gesture attached to a view and working.

Installing the Custom Gesture

Using your new DeleteGestureRecognizer is no different from the other recognizers we've worked with: we simply attach it to a view and define the action that is called when the view recognizes a gesture. We'll get to the action in a bit, but what view do we want to attach to?

If we attach to the individual bubbles, we'll need to start the delete gesture within the bubble itself for the touches to go to that view. It's more natural to perform the eraser-like gesture around the bubble image—not necessarily *within* it.

So, let's attach the delete gesture to the Bubbles5ViewController's view, which contains the bubbles, and then we can begin the gesture anywhere. Of course, at some point, we're going to have to figure out which image view to delete—but no worries there; we've already done something similar with our bubble tap gestures. First, let's check out the code to attach our gesture to the BubblesViewController's view.

gestures/Bubbles5/Classes/Bubbles5ViewController.m

```
- (void)viewDidLoad {
        [super viewDidLoad];

        // previous gesture code goes here

▶       DeleteGestureRecognizer *deleteRecognizer =
▶               [[DeleteGestureRecognizer alloc]
▶                       initWithTarget:self
▶                       action:@selector(handleDeleteFrom:)];
▶       [self.view addGestureRecognizer:deleteRecognizer];
▶       [deleteRecognizer release];
}
```

You've seen all this before: the only item of note is that we're going to use an action called handleDeleteFrom. Let's implement that:

gestures/Bubbles5/Classes/Bubbles5ViewController.m

```
- (void)handleDeleteFrom:(DeleteGestureRecognizer *)recognizer {
        if (recognizer.state == UIGestureRecognizerStateRecognized) {
                UIView *viewToDelete = [recognizer viewToDelete];
                [viewToDelete removeFromSuperview];
        }
}
```

This code is straightforward: we grab the view to be deleted from the recognizer, and then we simply remove it from the superview (our Bubbles5ViewController). There's only one problem. If you look back at the DeleteGestureRecognizer implementation, we never assigned a view to the recognizer's viewToDelete property. Now that we know where this view is being attached (to a view containing subviews of images to be deleted), we have a better idea of how to implement that. Here's a bit of new code for the DeleteGestureRecognizer's touchesMoved:withEvent: method:

gestures/Bubbles5/Classes/DeleteGestureRecognizer.m

```
- (void)touchesMoved:(NSSet *)touches withEvent:(UIEvent *)event {
        [super touchesMoved:touches withEvent:event];

        if (self.state == UIGestureRecognizerStateFailed) return;

        CGPoint nowPoint = [[touches anyObject] locationInView:self.view];
        CGPoint prevPoint = [[touches anyObject] previousLocationInView:self.view]

        if (strokeMovingUp == YES) {
                if (nowPoint.y < prevPoint.y ) {
                        strokeMovingUp = NO;
                        touchChangedDirection++;
                }
```

```
        } else if (nowPoint.y > prevPoint.y ) {
                strokeMovingUp = YES;
                touchChangedDirection++;
        }

        if (viewToDelete == nil) {
                UIView *hit = [self.view hitTest:nowPoint withEvent:nil];
                if (hit != nil && hit != self.view) {
                        self.viewToDelete = hit;
                }
        }
}
```

Let's walk through this. If viewToDelete hasn't already been determined, we take the current location of the user's finger at each point as it is moving, and we perform a hit test on the controller's view. Remember, the hit test gives us the deepest view in the view hierarchy that contains this location. If there is no view or the view is just the controller's view, then we haven't found an image view. Otherwise, if we have, we've located the view the user's finger is erasing. That's our view, so we assign it to viewToDelete.

That's our last piece of code. Our bubble wrap application is ready to be compiled and test-driven, so create some bubbles and then delete them.

Letting the Delete Recognizer Sink In

We just wrote a custom recognizer and integrated it into our bubble wrap application in surprisingly few lines of code. That said, there's a lot of thinking and technology behind that little implementation. Let's quickly review: we created a recognizer that tracks a user's single finger motion up and down the y-axis. If more than one finger is used, we enter the failed state, and reset is called to prepare the recognizer to try on the next set of Multi-Touch events. If the user lifts his fingers before the motion changes direction three or more times, we also enter the failed state. But if the user does everything as expected, we enter the recognized state, and the UIGestureRecognizer superclass, behind the scenes, takes care of sending the action message to our target (remember the target is the object waiting to be notified if the gesture is recognized). Further, our code tracks the user's motion, and as soon as his finger passes over a UIImageView, we keep a reference to that view as the view to be deleted, should the gesture pass recognition.

The code isn't perfect. For one thing, this isn't the most sophisticated logic for the gesture—but does it need to be? Sometimes simple heuristics work surprisingly well. What if a few bubbles are close to each other? Does this code delete them all? No—it just deletes the first UIImageView that the user's finger passes over. How can we fix this? And finally, what if the application confuses a swipe and a delete? It's now time to fix that.

3.7 What's That Popping Sound?

Do you find it as unsatisfying as we do that there is no sound when we pop a bubble? Let's add one. If you open the Bubbles5conflict project (the name comes from the topic of our next section), you'll find we've already added a bubble.aif sound for you. To get your code playing this audio file when the bubble is popped on the screen, let's use the AVAudioPlayer class, which is a good choice for sounds located in the bundle (instead of, say, streamed over the network) that we just need to play without any need for audio processing or mixing.

To use the AVAudioPlayer class, you'll need to add the AVFoundation framework to your project and include the following import in your Bubbles5ViewController.h header file:

```
#import <AVFoundation/AVFoundation.h>
```

While you're there, add an instance variable for the player itself:

```
AVAudioPlayer *player;
```

And method declarations:

```
-(void)preparePopSound;
-(void)makePopSound;
```

We're going to use the first method to set up the audio player, and we're going to call the second method any time we want to hear the pop sound. Let's define the preparePopSound method now:

gestures/Bubbles5conflict/Classes/Bubbles5ViewController.m
```
-(void)preparePopSound {
        NSURL *url = [NSURL fileURLWithPath:
                [NSString stringWithFormat:@"%@/bubble.aif",
                [[NSBundle mainBundle] resourcePath]]];

        NSError *error;
        player = [[AVAudioPlayer alloc]
                        initWithContentsOfURL:url error:&error];
        player.numberOfLoops = 0;
}
```

Here we're first creating an NSURL object that points to the bubble.aif file in the bundle. We're then instantiating an AVAudioPlayer to play that URL and setting its number of times (loops) to play to zero, which means it won't repeat after playing once.

Now let's take a look at the makePopSound: method:

gestures/Bubbles5conflict/Classes/Bubbles5ViewController.m

```
-(void)makePopSound {
        [player play];
}
```

It doesn't get any easier than that. We just ask the player to play the sound.

Now you just need to find a place to call both methods. For preparePop-Sound:, you can place that method anywhere in the viewDidLoad: method of Bubbles5ViewController.m. For the makePopSound:, we just need to add that to the code where it's determined the bubble has been popped, in handleTapFrom:. Here's how:

gestures/Bubbles5conflict/Classes/Bubbles5ViewController.m

```
- (void)handleTapFrom:(UITapGestureRecognizer *)recognizer {
        CGPoint location = [recognizer locationInView:self.view];

        UIView *hitView = [self.view hitTest:location withEvent:nil];
        if ([hitView isKindOfClass:[UIImageView class]]) {
                [(UIImageView *)hitView
                 setImage:[UIImage imageNamed:@"popped.png"]];
                [self makePopSound];
        } else {
                //rest of handleTapFrom goes here
        }

}
```

Here once we've determined the hit view is a bubble, we change its image to the popped image, and then we call makePopSound:. Add this to your code, and give it a try. Ah, that's much more satisfying, isn't it?

You might have noticed you can pop a bubble multiple times—we'll leave that to you to solve. Now, let's get back to gestures.

3.8 Competing Recognizers

Run your bubbles application again, and try to delete a bubble using the gesture we've shown in Figure 3.6, on the next page; here we're attempting a delete gesture, but we're doing it after sliding one finger

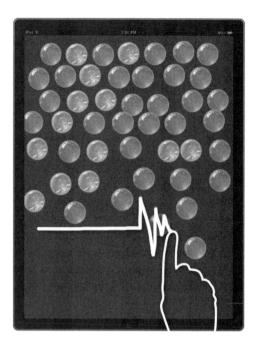

Figure 3.6: COMPETING DELETE AND SWIPE GESTURES

to the right quite a distance. At first this looks like a swipe gesture, but then we perform the necessary movements to make it a deletion gesture—at least that's how we think it should work. But if your experience is like ours, you'll see that this often (if not always) gets recognized as a swipe gesture, and your entire board is erased.

To finish off this chapter, we're going to fix this behavior by making sure the delete gesture has a chance to be recognized before the swipe gesture completes. To understand how this works, we first need to talk about how two gestures on the same view operate. In our case, we have several gestures installed on our main view: a single tap, a swipe gesture, and our custom delete gesture. As touch events are received, they are routed to all three of these recognizers until one of them recognizes its respective gesture. In our example, the swipe gesture sees touch events that tell it there is a swipe, and it recognizes the swipe before we even start the delete part of our gestures. In some implementations, this may actually be the behavior you want, but in this example, it feels wrong, so we want to alter the recognizers a bit to allow a single delete to take precedence over the swipe gesture.

To solve this problem, we're going to introduce a new method, require-GestureRecognizerToFail:, of the UIGestureRecognizer base class, which allows us to require that one recognizer fail before another gets its chance at recognizing a Multi-Touch stream of events.

The requireGestureRecognizerToFail: method can be called on any recognizer and has one parameter: another recognizer. Here's an example of how we use it:

```
[secondRecognizer requireGestureRecognizerToFail:firstRecognizer]
```

The method causes the secondRecognizer to stay in its UIGestureRecognizerStatePossible state until the firstRecognizer reaches its UIGestureRecognizerStateFailed state. If the firstRecognizer doesn't and instead reaches either the UIGestureRecognizerStateRecognized or UIGestureRecognizerStateBegan state, then the secondRecognizer changes its state to UIGestureRecognizerStateFailed. In the case where the firstRecognizer reaches its UIGestureRecognizerStateFailed state, then the secondRecognizer gets its chance at recognizing the Multi-Touch events.

Given that knowledge, we need to make sure that our delete recognizer gets its chance at recognizing the gesture before the swipe recognizer begins its examination of the gestures. To do that we're going to want to call the requireGestureRecognizerToFail: method on the swipe gesture recognizer and pass it the delete recognizer.

After all this discussion, developing the code is actually quite easy—all you need to do is add one line just below the creation of the swipe and delete gestures in viewDidLoad:

gestures/Bubbles5conflict/Classes/Bubbles5ViewController.m

```
- (void)viewDidLoad {
        [super viewDidLoad];

        // previous gesture code goes here


        DeleteGestureRecognizer *deleteRecognizer =
                [[DeleteGestureRecognizer alloc]
                        initWithTarget:self
                        action:@selector(handleDeleteFrom:)];
        [self.view addGestureRecognizer:deleteRecognizer];

▶       [swipeRecognizer requireGestureRecognizerToFail:deleteRecognizer];
▶       [deleteRecognizer release];
▶       [swipeRecognizer release];
}
```

> **Extra Credit: Popping a Popped Bubble?**
>
> As implemented, you can pop a popped bubble. Go ahead, try it. See!
>
> Your extra credit is to alter the code slightly to make sure that can't happen. How are you going to do it?

Here, as we've already discussed, we're telling the swipeRecognizer that the deleteRecognizer needs to fail before it can begin trying to recognize the gesture. Note that you should also move the release of the two gestures below the requireGestureRecognizerToFail: method. Compile your code and give it a try.

3.9 Summary

In this chapter, we've generated only a small amount of actual code, and yet, although our example is simple, we've demonstrated some powerful uses of gestures. You are going to find it is that easy to add the same behavior into your own applications.

Although we've hit all the high points of Apple's new gesture APIs in this chapter, if you want to more precisely control the way views, gestures, and multiple gestures behave, you may want to explore the additional, low-level calls that allow you to fine-tune these behaviors (see the *iPad Programming Guide* [App10b] for more details). However, for most common uses, you won't need to go that deep. Overall, you'll find that the new gesture APIs significantly reduce the complexity of adding gestures to your views in most cases, and you're probably already discovering that gestures are a vital part of designing experiences for the iPad.

Chapter 4

Popovers and Modal Dialog Boxes

Sometimes the user will need to enter more information than can be communicated in a single gesture. Maybe they'll need to select from a list of options to set the color of a component, the font of the text, or the web page to load.

In this chapter, we'll create a simple app that features a storage container for which users can select the color. That's not the world's most exciting app—we'll spice it up at the end by adding a panel to allow users to move the container around the screen.

The users select the container by tapping it, but then what? Using simple gestures, we could cycle through a predefined set of colors. That's not a lot of fun. In an iPhone application, we would usually push a modal view onto the screen and use it to enter the custom information. We can use the same technique on the iPad. We'll begin this chapter with a look at how to do that and how to take advantage of some of the iPad-specific options for modal views.[1]

Modal views aren't always the best choice. We could provide these same choices using the new iPad popover that you saw in Chapter 2, *Introducing Split Views*. It turns out that *how* we implement these two options is fairly similar. The main thing you need to determine is *when* it makes sense to use a modal view and when it makes sense to use a popover. In this chapter, we'll cover both the how and the when. We'll also take some time to understand what goes on behind the scenes with the split view controller to set up the popover we saw in the portrait view.

---

1. Recall that a modal view requires that you perform an action and dismiss that view before you can interact with any other aspect of the application.

The core technique for using modal views or popovers is similar:

1. Listen for an event. We'll listen for a tap on our cargo container and for a button press.

2. Create a view controller and an associated nib containing the contents of the view that will be displayed either modally or in a popover.

3. When the event is received, display the modal view or popover.

4. Respond to user interaction with the controller, and dismiss it when the user is done with it.

Let's get started.

4.1 Responding to Touch

We've gotten you started with a sample project in the code download. Open the project in the Cargo1 folder, and you'll find a view-based iPad application named Cargo.

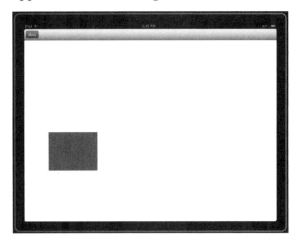

All we've done so far is open the CargoViewController nib, add a subview with a red background to represent our cargo container, and place a toolbar with a single Move button on it.

Let's attach the tap gesture to our cargo container. Add an outlet named cargoView to CargoViewController.h, and wire it to your cargo container. Use the technique you learned in Section 3.2, *Attaching the Gesture to a View*, to register the method named cargoContainerDidGetTapped for taps on the cargo container. We autorelease the gesture recognizer as soon as we create it because the cargoView holds a reference to it.

Popover/Cargo2/Classes/CargoViewController.m

```
- (void)viewDidLoad {
    [super viewDidLoad];
►   [cargoView addGestureRecognizer:
►           [[[UITapGestureRecognizer alloc]
►               initWithTarget:self
►                   action:@selector(cargoContainerDidGetTapped)]
►                                           autorelease]];
}
```

In this first implementation, we'll just change the color every time the user taps the container:

Popover/Cargo2/Classes/CargoViewController.m

```
-(void) cargoContainerDidGetTapped {
    cargoView.backgroundColor = [UIColor colorWithRed:(random()%3)/3.0
                                        green:(random()%3)/3.0
                                         blue:(random()%3)/3.0
                                        alpha:1];
}
```

Pretty cool. Now the app responds to touch. The cargo container's color changes somewhat randomly when it is touched. Next let's push a modal view to provide the user with a small palette of colors to choose from.

4.2 Creating the Color Controller

Whether we are enabling color selection using a modal view or using a popover, we create a new view controller along with a new view-based nib. Create a new class named CargoColorChooser that is a UIViewController subclass; check the boxes so it is targeted for iPad and a nib is also generated for the user interface.

Feel free to grab the CargoColorChooser nib from the Cargo3 folder, or set it up yourself. The view is 200×240 with a label on top, six 40×40 buttons in two rows, and a button on the bottom.[2]

---

2. To get the square buttons, drag UIViews out of the Library, place them, color them, and then change their class to UIButton.

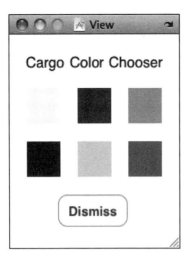

See that Dismiss button at the bottom of the view? That's a major differ-ence between the controller views you'll use for a modal view and those that you'll use for a popover. The user expects to dismiss a popover by completing an action or by touching the screen off the popover. A modal view must provide the user with a way to dismiss it, since no other input can occur while the modal view is in focus.

The CargoColorChooser class needs to provide actions for the Dismiss and the color buttons, and it needs to communicate with the cargo UIView object. Add this outlet and two actions to CargoColorChooser.h:

`Popover/Cargo4/Classes/CargoColorChooser.h`

```
#import <UIKit/UIKit.h>

@interface CargoColorChooser : UIViewController {
    IBOutlet UIView *cargoView;
}
-(IBAction) dismiss;
-(IBAction) setCargoColor:(id)sender;
@end
```

The CargoColorChooser object is your bridge between the main appli-cation view and the modal dialog box; it needs a foot in both worlds. It is already the File's Owner in the CargoColorChooser nib, so you can connect your buttons to the dismiss and setCargoColor: actions. When connecting, choose the Touch Up Inside event to trigger the actions.

Drag an instance of CargoColorChooser into the CargoViewController nib, and connect the cargoView outlet.[3] Check the Attributes inspector for

---

3. Remember that since CargoColorChooser is a class that we created ourselves, you'll find it in the Library on the Classes tab.

the CargoColorChooser and make sure that the checkbox for Resize View from NIB is unchecked. Add an outlet in CargoViewController.h of type CargoColorChooser named cargoColorChooser. Connect this outlet to the CargoColorChooser object in the CargoViewController nib.

So far, you'll essentially use the same setup whether you are planning on using a modal dialog box or a popover. Next, let's implement the modal dialog box.

4.3 Pushing Modal Views

We have all the pieces assembled; now let's add some finishing touches and push our modal view. Currently, the cargoContainerDidGetTapped method in CargoViewController.m switches the color of the cargo container.

Change the implementation to this to open the modal view:

Popover/Cargo5/Classes/CargoViewController.m

```
-(void) cargoContainerDidGetTapped {
    [self presentModalViewController:cargoColorChooser animated:YES];
}
```

Build and run. Now when you tap the cargo container, the modal view should animate up from the bottom and fill the screen.

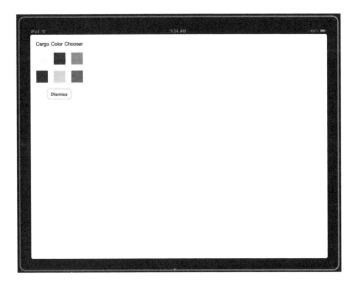

It's almost embarrassing how easy this is.

> ### Preparing and Finishing
>
> Presenting a modal view or a popover is like the job of house painters. Although they need to take care in applying the final coat, the real work is done in preparing the surface and getting everything ready for the final coat. The code for presenting and dismissing our view is fairly concise. Most of the work involves preparing the controller and nib that will be displayed.

We also need to dismiss the modal view when the user clicks the Dismiss button. We'll do that in the dismiss action in CargoColorChooser.m.

Popover/Cargo5/Classes/CargoColorChooser.m

```
-(IBAction) dismiss {
    [self dismissModalViewControllerAnimated:YES];
}
```

Finally, let's implement the action to change the cargo container's color based on the user's selection in the modal view.

Popover/Cargo5/Classes/CargoColorChooser.m

```
-(IBAction) setCargoColor:(id)sender{
    cargoView.backgroundColor = ((UIView *) sender).backgroundColor;
}
```

Now when you build and run, you can tap the cargo container to bring up the modal view, select a color, and dismiss the modal view to see your cargo container with its new color.

Notice that even though we created a very small view in the CargoColorChooser nib, the modal view takes up the entire screen. With the iPad, you can select other options that change the size of the modal view being displayed. You can set the modalPresentationStyle property of the view controller that will be presented. For example, add the following highlighted line to the cargoContainerDidGetTapped implementation:

Popover/Cargo6/Classes/CargoViewController.m

```
-(void) cargoContainerDidGetTapped {
▶   cargoColorChooser.modalPresentationStyle = UIModalPresentationFormSheet;
    [self presentModalViewController:cargoColorChooser animated:YES];
}
```

The UIModalPresentationFormSheet option results in a smaller modal view centered on the screen with the background dimmed to let the users know that they aren't supposed to be able to interact with anything not on the modal view.

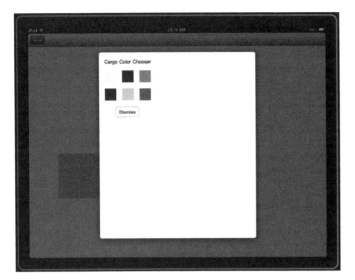

Now when the users select other colors, they see the results immediately, instead of waiting until the screen is dismissed. This is, of course, not guaranteed. If the cargo container had been placed in the center of the screen, even this smaller modal view would obscure it. One solution is to set the CargoColorChooser's view to have a clear background color. A better solution in our case is to use a popover.

4.4 Streamlining the Controller

Users should never be required to use some sort of button to dismiss a popover. The popover should disappear when the users tap the screen outside of the popover; or, if it is natural to do so, the popover can disappear after the users complete an action. In our example, we could dismiss the popover when the users select a color—or we could leave it up so that they can select a color, look at the result, and perhaps select another color. In each situation, consider what behavior best matches the users' expectations.

In either case, Apple's *iPad Human Interface Guidelines* [App10a] is clear about not including a button to dismiss a popover. Remove the Dismiss button from our CargoColorChooser's view. While you're at it, remove the dismiss action from the CargoColorChooser class.

Most of the remaining decisions are a matter of taste. We're going to set the popover to appear next to the cargo container with an arrow pointing at the container. We can probably eliminate the label Cargo Color Chooser and just display the six colored buttons. You may want to resize the buttons or arrange them in a single column. We'll remove the label and reduce the view containing the buttons to fit more snugly around them.

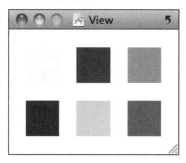

Before we head off to create our popover, run this code as it is to see the difference between what we need to present in a modal view and what we need to present in a popover. Presenting these six colored squares without any context just doesn't work in a modal view. There's also no way to leave the modal view once we're in it. On the other hand, as we'll soon see, the look and feel works great in a popover.

4.5 Displaying a Popover

It's slightly more complicated to display a popover than a modal view. We can customize the controller in more ways to describe where it is in relation to the object the user taps to present it.

First we'll create a UIPopoverController. To configure the init, we have to tell it which view controller it will be using for its content. A popover controller is not itself a view controller; it hosts a view controller. Here we've set the popoverContentSize property so that the popover is the same size as the view we configured in the CargoColorChooser nib.

When it's time to present the popover, we need to specify the visual element the user tapped so that the arrow is drawn back from the popover to that element. In fact, you may be displaying a popover to customize a specific portion of the view you are pointing at. You can specify a specific region in that view by setting the rectangle you're targeting. In our case, we're modifying the entire cargo container, so we set the rectangle to be cargoView.bounds.

Popover/Cargo8/Classes/CargoViewController.m

```
-(void) cargoContainerDidGetTapped {
    UIPopoverController *popover = [[UIPopoverController alloc]
                        initWithContentViewController:cargoColorChooser];
    popover.popoverContentSize = cargoColorChooser.view.frame.size;
    [popover presentPopoverFromRect:cargoView.bounds
                        inView:cargoView
            permittedArrowDirections:UIPopoverArrowDirectionAny animated:YES];
}
```

Build and run, and you should see something like this when you click
the cargo container:

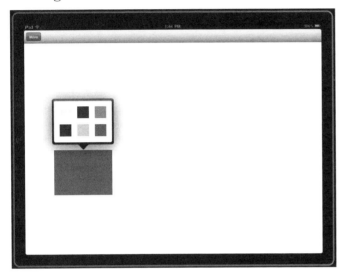

We didn't specify the direction of the arrow. For permittedArrowDirections,
we passed in the value UIPopoverArrowDirectionAny. Use this option whenever you can to let the system figure out where best to draw the popover.
If there's a strong reason for specifying a particular orientation, then it's
a good idea to offer options. So, for example, here we indicate that it's
OK to draw the popover on the left or the right of the view:

Popover/Cargo8a/Classes/CargoViewController.m

```
-(void) cargoContainerDidGetTapped {
    UIPopoverController *popover = [[UIPopoverController alloc]
                        initWithContentViewController:cargoColorChooser];
    popover.popoverContentSize = cargoColorChooser.view.frame.size;
    [popover presentPopoverFromRect:cargoView.bounds
                        inView:cargoView
            permittedArrowDirections:UIPopoverArrowDirectionLeft +
                                    UIPopoverArrowDirectionRight
                        animated:YES];
}
```

In this case, the container is too close to the left edge, so the popover is drawn to the right. It's a matter of taste, but this particular popover feels better presented next to the view rather than above or below it.

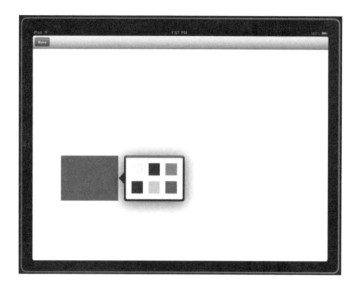

Now that we've made the popover appear, let's make it disappear. Currently, the user can get the popover to disappear by clicking anywhere on the screen. It wouldn't take very much to get the popover to disappear whenever a color is selected.

You're going to need a handle back to the popover controller. Add a property named popoverController of type UIPopoverController to the Cargo-ColorChooser class. Set the property by adding the highlighted line below to the cargoContainerDidGetTapped method in CargoViewController.m:

Popover/Cargo9/Classes/CargoViewController.m

```
-(void) cargoContainerDidGetTapped {
    UIPopoverController *popover = [[UIPopoverController alloc]
                        initWithContentViewController:cargoColorChooser];
    popover.popoverContentSize = cargoColorChooser.view.frame.size;
    cargoColorChooser.popoverController = popover;
    [popover presentPopoverFromRect:cargoView.bounds
                        inView:cargoView
            permittedArrowDirections:UIPopoverArrowDirectionLeft +
        UIPopoverArrowDirectionRight
                        animated:YES];
}
```

Dismiss the popover controller after the color is selected:

Popover/Cargo9/Classes/CargoColorChooser.m

```
-(IBAction) setCargoColor:(id)sender{
    cargoView.backgroundColor = ((UIView *) sender).backgroundColor;
    [self.popoverController dismissPopoverAnimated:YES];
}
```

4.6 Revisiting the Split View and Popovers

Think back to when we added a button to our detail view when the split view transitioned from landscape to portrait mode back in Section 2.8, *Adding a Popover*. Now you are in a position to better understand what's going on.

In our example, the RootViewController was hidden as the iPad rotated, so we want to stick its contents inside the popover that will appear when the button in the toolbar is pressed.

As the iPad rotates into the portrait orientation, this delegate method is called:

SplitVC/DailyShootiPad/Classes/DetailViewController.m

```
- (void)splitViewController: (UISplitViewController*)svc
      willHideViewController:(UIViewController *)aViewController
          withBarButtonItem:(UIBarButtonItem*)barButtonItem
         forPopoverController: (UIPopoverController*)pc {
    barButtonItem.title = aViewController.title;
    NSMutableArray *items = [[toolbar items] mutableCopy];
    [items insertObject:barButtonItem atIndex:0];
    [toolbar setItems:items animated:YES];
    [items release];
    self.popoverController = pc;
}
```

This method gives us a handle to everything we need, but most of the work is done somewhere else. The body of the method mainly consists of configuring the bar button item and adding it to the toolbar. Before this method is called, the contents of the popover are set to be the view controller that is being hidden. As a result, we saw that the contents of the RootViewController magically appeared when the button was pressed.

It actually doesn't take very much for us to attach a popover to a button ourselves. Let's do that next.

4.7 Popovers from Buttons

We saw that our running example of setting the color of the cargo container works equally well from a modal view or from a popover. Generally, if we don't need a modal view, we shouldn't use one. In other words, we'd clearly favor using the popover in this example. Sometimes the choice is much clearer. Imagine we have a popover controller that can be used to move the container around the screen.

The next stage of our project is in the Cargo10 folder. You'll find an additional view controller named CarDriver and the corresponding nib file. The view in the nib looks like this:

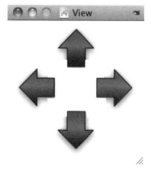

Let's attach this to the Move button.

Add an outlet for the CarDriver named carDriver to the CargoViewController class. Drag an instance of CarDriver into the CargoViewController nib, and connect the outlet to it. Make sure that the checkbox for the CarDriver's Resize View from NIB is unchecked.

We'll need an action that is invoked when the button is pressed. Declare an IBAction named showDriveControls: in CargoViewController.h. In fact, because this is the last thing we're adding to the CargoViewController header file, it's probably a good time to take a look at it in its entirety—there is not much required to support the cargo container and two popovers.

Popover/Cargo11/Classes/CargoViewController.h

```
#import <UIKit/UIKit.h>
@class CargoColorChooser;
@class CarDriver;

@interface CargoViewController : UIViewController {
    IBOutlet UIView *cargoView;
    IBOutlet CargoColorChooser *cargoColorChooser;
    IBOutlet CarDriver *carDriver;
}
-(IBAction) showDriveControls:(id)sender;
@end
```

Connect the button to the action, and then implement the action like this:

Popover/Cargo11/Classes/CargoViewController.m

```
-(IBAction)showDriveControls:(id)sender {
    UIPopoverController *controls = [[UIPopoverController alloc]
                            initWithContentViewController:carDriver];
    controls.popoverContentSize = carDriver.view.frame.size;
    [controls presentPopoverFromBarButtonItem:sender
                permittedArrowDirections:UIPopoverArrowDirectionAny
                                animated:YES];
}
```

As before, we instantiate the popover controller and assign it the contents of a particular view controller, in this case carDriver. Next, we set the size of the popover. You may want to see what happens if you leave this line out. Finally, we present the popover and specify the bar button that it is associated with so that the arrow can point back at the button the user pressed to bring up the popover.

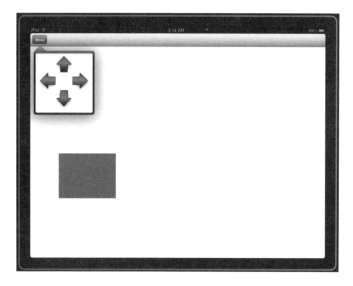

As an exercise, respond to taps on the four arrows to make the cargo container move in the direction of the arrow being tapped. A possible solution is provided in the code download in Cargo12.

What happens if you press the button when the popover is already visible? The showDriveControls method is called again, which contains the code for creating the popover controller and displaying it. You can see the problem with this if you press the button. Press the button again. Now click something else to dismiss the popover. You'll see this empty popover in the top left.

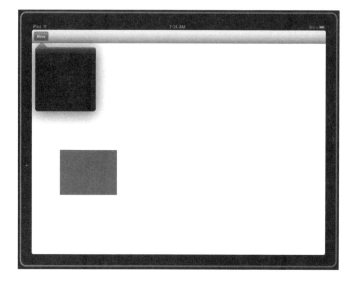

That's not right. What you want is for the the popover to be dismissed if you press the button a second time. You can accomplish this by adding an instance variable named driveControls of type UIPopoverController to CargoViewController.h. Change the name of the showDriveControls: method to showOrHideDriveControls:, and fix the connection in the nib.

Implement showOrHideDriveControls: to toggle the popover. If the controller exists, dismiss the popover, and nil out the controller. If the controller doesn't exist, create, configure, and display it.

We also have to take care of the case where the user dismisses the drive controls by clicking elsewhere on the screen. For this case, we'll set the CargoViewController object to be the delegate for the popover controller. You'll need to add the declaration of the UIPopoverControllerDelegate protocol to CargoViewController.h. When the delegate method popoverControllerDidDismissPopover: method is called, we'll delete the drive control popover controller.

Popover/Cargo13/Classes/CargoViewController.m

```
-(IBAction)showOrHideDriveControls:(id)sender {
    if (driveControls) {
        [driveControls dismissPopoverAnimated:YES];
        driveControls = nil;
    } else {
    driveControls = [[UIPopoverController alloc]
                            initWithContentViewController:carDriver];
    driveControls.popoverContentSize = carDriver.view.frame.size;
    [driveControls presentPopoverFromBarButtonItem:sender
                permittedArrowDirections:UIPopoverArrowDirectionAny
                            animated:YES];
    driveControls.delegate = self;
    }
}
- (void)popoverControllerDidDismissPopover:
                    (UIPopoverController *)popoverController {
    driveControls = nil;
}
```

4.8 Changing Orientations

The first time we looked at popovers in Chapter 2, *Introducing Split Views*, on page 23, we implemented delegate methods to respond to the user rotating the device. In our current example, we don't have a split view, but we may want to present visual components in different locations or with different dimensions depending on whether the user is holding the iPad horizontally or vertically.

In our example, there really aren't any visual elements that need to be arranged, so we'll add four colored square UIViews so that you can see how the technique would work. Place a UIView of size 100 by 100 in each corner, and set each background color to a different color.

Use the Size inspector to set the cargoView to maintain its distance from each side as the device is rotated. Create outlets in the CargoViewController named corner1, corner2, corner3, and corner4. When the app runs, we'll exchange the squares that are diagonally opposite each other when the device rotates. The starting position might look something like this:

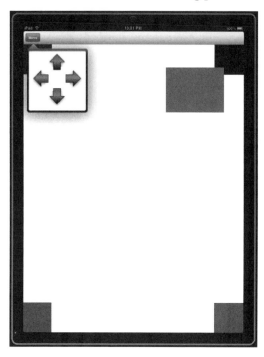

The key to coordinating the animation is to add any additional animations to the willAnimateRotationToInterfaceOrientation:duration: method in the view controller.[4]

Popover/Cargo14/Classes/CargoViewController.m

```
- (void)willAnimateRotationToInterfaceOrientation:
                        (UIInterfaceOrientation)interfaceOrientation
                             duration:(NSTimeInterval)duration {
```

---

4. In this simple example, we've hard-coded the dimensions of the view in each orientation and of the corners. In an application you will be maintaining over time, you would use calls to the system and constants, respectively. You'll see an example of this in Section 5.5, *Using Keyboard Notifications*, on page 100.

```
    if (interfaceOrientation == UIInterfaceOrientationPortrait ||
        interfaceOrientation == UIInterfaceOrientationPortraitUpsideDown) {
        corner1.frame = CGRectMake(0, 44, 100, 100);
        corner2.frame = CGRectMake(668, 44, 100, 100);
        corner3.frame = CGRectMake(0, 904, 100, 100);
        corner4.frame = CGRectMake(668, 904, 100, 100);
    } else {
        corner4.frame = CGRectMake(0, 44, 100, 100);
        corner3.frame = CGRectMake(924, 44, 100, 100);
        corner2.frame = CGRectMake(0, 648, 100, 100);
        corner1.frame = CGRectMake(924, 648, 100, 100);
    }
}
```

The ending position might look something like this:

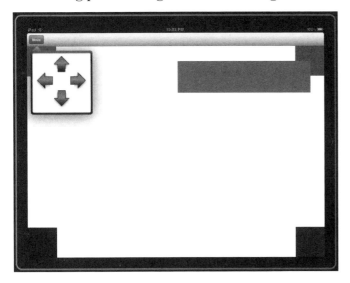

We've really only specified the beginning and ending positions of each of the corner blocks. To get the full effect, run the animation by rotating the iPad in the simulator or on the device. The popover will fade out, and the four corners will exchange their positions at the same time that the cargoView resizes.

This animation looks better if we keep our cargoView on top, so add this line to the viewDidLoad method in CargoViewController.m:

Popover/Cargo14/Classes/CargoViewController.m

```
[self.view bringSubviewToFront:cargoView];
```

Throughout your iPad development, remember that you need to consider how best to present your app in each orientation. In this section, you saw a simple example of how to smoothly move and resize elements as the user rotates the device. This sort of animation is not gratuitous (OK, it was in this example). You are helping the user follow the item they are currently most interested in. You are helping them make the transition from one orientation to another.

4.9 Summary

In this chapter, we looked at variations on modal views and popovers. We created a modal view that obscured the entire screen and one that occupied the center while dimming the nonresponsive areas of the screen. We created popovers when a portion of a view is tapped and when a button is pressed. We examined how to arrange the popover differently with respect to the UI component that initiates the presentation of the popover. We saw how to dismiss the popover following a user action, and we communicated from the popover or modal view back to another object.

The basic pattern is one we'll use throughout our iPad programming: we created a nib and did most of the work in the view controller that acts as the File's Owner for that nib. When it is time to present a modal view or a popover, we need to make a few connections in each direction and bring up the new view containing the contents managed by our custom view controller. This is the same basic technique used to create custom table cells and other things.

Chapter 5

Custom Keyboards

Imagine that there was a version of Apple's Keynote or Pages application designed for the iPhone. What would it do? You could imagine viewing existing Pages documents or Keynote presentations, but it would be awfully hard to create new documents on such a small screen. You've always been able to enter text on your iPhone—how else are you going to enter a URL in Safari, enter an address in Maps, or reply to email in Mail? Although it works in a pinch, the iPhone is not going to be your go-to device for working with complicated documents.

The key problem is that your finger takes up a lot of the iPhone screen. As Craig Hockenberry writes, "The screen on the iPhone squeezes 160 pixels into every inch of display space—and you're using your finger to access that display. If you press your finger against the edge of a ruler, you'll see it uses somewhere between 1/4" and 1/2" at the point of contact. That corresponds to anywhere between 40 and 80 pixels of display space."[1]

That means the iPhone screen is roughly five fingers wide. Given that, it's amazing how easy it is to enter text on this pocket-sized device. You've seen how much bigger the iPad is than the iPhone, and one place that this really pays off is when using the soft keyboard. In this chapter, we'll see how easy it is to create a custom keyboard or to augment the existing keyboard using the text view's properties inputView and inputAccessoryView.

---

1. See http://www.alistapart.com/articles/putyourcontentinmypocket/. Since Craig made these comments, Apple has introduced iPhone 4 with twice the resolution. The numbers double, but the point remains that you are obscuring a lot of the display every time you touch the screen.

The iPad's size allows you to do more than just *view* documents on it. In portrait orientation, the screen is more than a dozen fingers wide. In landscape, you have room for even more fingers—if you had them.

On the iPad, you're going to want to create new documents and edit existing ones like you can in the iPad versions of Keynote, Pages, and Numbers. You won't be satisfied to merely view documents created elsewhere. You've already seen how to take advantage of the new techniques for gestures and how to use popovers. In this chapter, you'll learn how to offer custom text input.

5.1 Basic Text Input

Create a view-based iPad project, and name it Feelings. Add a text view to the FeelingsViewController nib. We'll use this text view to display emoticons that let people nearby know how you are feeling. We'll restrict ourselves to ;-), :-), :-(, and >:(.[2]

For effect you may want to set the background color of the text view to yellow, set the font to something big and bold like Helvetica bold 288, and make sure the text view is large enough to hold the angry emoticon. Really, that's all you need. Build and run, and you should be able to type in the emoticons.

---

2. These are wink, happy, sad, and angry, respectively.

At this point, the app is not a very good user experience. For example, type the angry emoticon. You have to change keyboards to enter the three symbols. You know from your time as an iPhone developer that it's best to choose the keyboard that most meets your users' needs. But if you look at the list of available keyboards, none of them really fits your needs.

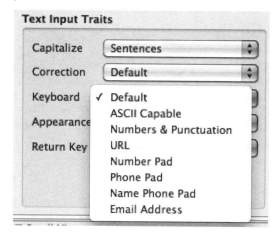

There are keyboards for entering words, numbers, URLs, and more, but there's nothing that helps us with emoticons. Let's create our own.

You'll use some of the same techniques that you use when you target the iPhone. It is still critical that you tailor the keyboard to the information that is being entered. Now you also have the option of replacing the keyboard with your own custom keyboard or of attaching your custom keyboard to the top of one of the standard ones. In this chapter, you'll see how easy it is for you to implement this.

5.2 Creating Custom Keyboards

We're going to create a custom keyboard for selecting emoticons. Our users will have to press only one button to express how they are feeling. To start with, we're going to need a new nib file that contains the view that will slide into view where we used to see the keyboard. Add a new file to the Resources group using the iPad's User Interface > View XIB template. Name it MoodKeyboard.

Select the view, and use the Attributes inspector to set the status bar to Unspecified. Use the Size inspector to size the view to be 768 pixels wide and 95 pixels high. Set the struts and springs so that the view remains anchored to the left, right, and bottom and so it grows horizontally. Set the view's background color to be a light shade of gray like the existing keyboard color. Change the File's Owner's type to be FeelingsViewController using the Identity inspector.

You'll need a PNG for each of the buttons. Feel free to use the ones you'll find in the code download in the directory Feelings2. We've designed the buttons to be custom buttons 75 by 75, evenly spaced, and centered on the view.

It's almost embarrassing to show you how easy it is to replace the standard keyboards with the one we just created. Add an outlet to FeelingsViewController.h for the view you just added to the new nib file and another outlet for the text view.

TextInput/Feelings2/Classes/FeelingsViewController.h

```
#import <UIKit/UIKit.h>

@interface FeelingsViewController : UIViewController {
}
@property(nonatomic,retain) IBOutlet UIView *moodKeyboard;
@property(nonatomic, retain) IBOutlet UITextView *textView;
@end
```

The FeelingsViewController has three outlets corresponding to properties we care about: moodKeyboard, textView, and view. The view should already be connected to the view in FeelingsViewController.xib. In that same nib, connect the textView outlet to the text view. Connect the moodKeyboard outlet to the view in MoodKeyboard.xib.

You have now made all the preparations; this is the only code that's needed to set up your custom keyboard. Add this implementation of the viewDidLoad method to FeelingsViewController.m.

TextInput/Feelings2/Classes/FeelingsViewController.m

```
- (void)viewDidLoad {
    [super viewDidLoad];
    [[NSBundle mainBundle] loadNibNamed:@"MoodKeyboard"
                                  owner:self
                                options:nil];
▶    self.textView.inputView = self.moodKeyboard;
}
```

After loading the nib and setting its File's Owner, the single highlighted line sets the text view's inputView property to be the view containing the custom buttons. Now let's make the buttons work.

5.3 Responding to Custom Buttons

We're going to enable the buttons so that when they are pressed, they do the work of multiple key presses. So, for example, here's what you should see when you press the angry button:

We are able to take advantage of one of the fundamental idioms in Cocoa programming. The FeelingsViewController object lives in two different nib files. We can add actions to it, connect the custom buttons to those actions in the MoodKeyboard nib, and then have it communicate with the text view through the outlet in the FeelingsViewController nib.

Add these actions to the FeelingsViewController header file:

TextInput/Feelings3/Classes/FeelingsViewController.h

```
-(IBAction) didTapWinkKey;
-(IBAction) didTapHappyKey;
-(IBAction) didTapSadKey;
-(IBAction) didTapAngryKey;
```

Wire these actions to the buttons, and implement them to set the text of the text view to the appropriate string and then to resign the first responder.

For example, when the user types the angry button, the didTapAngryKey method is called, which in turn calls the updateTextViewWithMood: method, passing in the string that corresponds to the angry emoticon.

TextInput/Feelings3/Classes/FeelingsViewController.m

```
-(void) updateTextViewWithMood:(NSString *) mood {
    self.textView.text = mood;
    [self.textView resignFirstResponder];
}
-(IBAction) didTapAngryKey{
    [self updateTextViewWithMood: @">:("];
}
```

Build and run. When you click the text view, the custom keyboard slides up and into place. Type any of the custom keys, and the corresponding text appears in the text view. Our custom keyboard lets us type one key instead of three.

5.4 Adding an Accessory View

You seldom need to type an emoticon all by itself. Mostly you use them to punctuate text. What we'd really like to do is display our custom keyboard along with the standard one. It turns out that all we need to do is change this single line of code:

TextInput/Feelings4/Classes/FeelingsViewController.m

```
- (void)viewDidLoad {
    [super viewDidLoad];
    [[NSBundle mainBundle] loadNibNamed:@"MoodKeyboard"
                                  owner:self
                                options:nil];
►   self.textView.inputAccessoryView = self.moodKeyboard;
}
```

Now when you select the text view, the standard keyboard slides into place with our custom keyboard on top. Think of our custom keyboard as an accessory for the standard keyboard. As you see in the code, all you need to do is set the text view's inputAccessoryView property instead of the inputView property.

We need to make some adjustments to our text view to highlight some additional work that needs to be done. Set the background color of the view to red. Change the font size for the text view to 72 from its current value of 288. Set the background color to white. Most importantly, change the size of the text view so that it almost covers the entire view.

Leave a margin of 20 pixels on each side so that you can see the text view framed by the red background color of the view.

Finally, adjust the updateTextViewWithMood: method so that it appends the mood to the existing text instead of replacing it and so that we no longer resign the first responder after entering a mood.

TextInput/Feelings4/Classes/FeelingsViewController.m

```
-(void) updateTextViewWithMood:(NSString *) mood {
    self.textView.text = [NSString stringWithFormat:@"%@ %@ ",
                                      self.textView.text, mood];
}
```

Build and run. Things look pretty good at first. There is, however, a little problem, as you can see here:

The bottom of the text view is hidden by the keyboard. If you keep typing, you'll find that the characters you are typing aren't visible. We need to resize the text view when the keyboard appears and disappears.

5.5 Using Keyboard Notifications

Remember that there is information whizzing around behind the scenes all the time. Notifications are sent when it's time for the keyboard to appear or hide. We just need to register to listen for them.[3] In view-DidLoad, we'll register for UIKeyboardWillShowNotification and UIKeyboard-WillHideNotification and specify the methods that will be called when we receive the notifications.

TextInput/Feelings5/Classes/FeelingsViewController.m

```
- (void)viewDidLoad {
    [super viewDidLoad];
    [[NSNotificationCenter defaultCenter]
                        addObserver:self
                           selector:@selector(keyboardWillAppear:)
                               name:UIKeyboardWillShowNotification
                             object:nil];
    [[NSNotificationCenter defaultCenter]
                        addObserver:self
                           selector:@selector(keyboardWillDisappear:)
                               name:UIKeyboardWillHideNotification
                             object:nil];
    [[NSBundle mainBundle] loadNibNamed:@"MoodKeyboard"
                                  owner:self
                                options:nil];
    self.textView.inputAccessoryView = self.moodKeyboard;
}
```

Here we've registered with the default notification center to be notified when the UIKeyboardWillShowNotification is issued. We've set this instance of the FeelingsViewController (that is, self) as the observer and specified that the message keyboardWillAppear: will be sent. In other words, whenever there is a UIKeyboardWillShowNotification, the default notification center will send a message that looks something like this:

```
[myFeelingsViewController keyboardWillAppear:notification];
```

We need to implement keyboardWillAppear: and the corresponding keyboardWillDisappear: methods. For now, let's just implement the two methods by logging the notifications to see what's available to us:

TextInput/Feelings5/Classes/FeelingsViewController.m

```
-(void)keyboardWillAppear:(NSNotification *)notification {
    NSLog(@"Keyboard will appear:\n %@", notification);
}
```

---

3. If you don't remember how to work with notifications, you'll find an introduction and examples in *Cocoa Programming: A Quick-Start Guide for Developers* [Ste09].

```
-(void)keyboardWillDisappear:(NSNotification *) notification {
    NSLog(@"Keyboard will disappear:\n %@", notification);
}
```

Build and run. When you tap the text view, you'll see something like this as part of the log:[4]

```
Keyboard will appear:
 NSConcreteNotification 0x51195a0 {name = UIKeyboardWillShowNotification;
 userInfo = {
    UIKeyboardAnimationCurveUserInfoKey = 0;
    UIKeyboardAnimationDurationUserInfoKey = 0.300000011920929;
    UIKeyboardBoundsUserInfoKey = NSRect: {{0, 0}, {768, 359}};
    UIKeyboardCenterBeginUserInfoKey = NSPoint: {384, 1203.5};
    UIKeyboardCenterEndUserInfoKey = NSPoint: {384, 844.5};
    UIKeyboardFrameBeginUserInfoKey = NSRect: {{0, 1024}, {768, 359}};
    UIKeyboardFrameEndUserInfoKey = NSRect: {{0, 665}, {768, 359}};
}}
```

To dismiss the keyboard, tap the key in the lower-right corner of the default keyboard, and you'll see the corresponding information for the UIKeyboardWillHideNotification. In both cases, the notification consists of the name of the notification and a userInfo dictionary. The userInfo tells us the time it will take to animate the keyboard on or off the screen. It also contains information about the geometry of the keyboard that we can use to animate our text view along with the keyboard.

5.6 Animating the Text View

We're going to use the information in the userInfo dictionary to animate and resize the text view in sync with the keyboard and accessory.

We have two things to take care of during the text view resizing. We want to make sure that the duration of the text view animation is the same as the time it takes to slide the keyboard in and out. While we're at it, we can ensure that we use the same animation curve that the keyboard uses so that we match the animation exactly.

TextInput/Feelings6/Classes/FeelingsViewController.m

```
-(void) matchAnimationTo:(NSDictionary *) userInfo {
    [UIView setAnimationDuration:
        [[userInfo objectForKey:UIKeyboardAnimationDurationUserInfoKey]
                doubleValue]];
```

---

4. These messages are written to the console, which you can access from the Xcode menu item Run > Console.

```
    [UIView setAnimationCurve:
       [[userInfo objectForKey:UIKeyboardAnimationCurveUserInfoKey]
                    intValue]];
}
```

We also need to adjust the text view by the height of the keyboard and accessory. First, we'll calculate the ending height of the keyboard:

TextInput/Feelings6/Classes/FeelingsViewController.m

```
-(CGFloat) keyboardEndingFrameHeight:(NSDictionary *) userInfo {
    CGRect keyboardEndingUncorrectedFrame =
        [[ userInfo objectForKey:UIKeyboardFrameEndUserInfoKey ]
                   CGRectValue];
    CGRect keyboardEndingFrame =
        [self.view convertRect:keyboardEndingUncorrectedFrame
                   fromView:nil];
    return keyboardEndingFrame.size.height;
}
```

Note that we had to use the method convertRect:fromView: to convert the keyboard ending rectangle that we get from the entry UIKeyboard-FrameEndUserInfoKey. The rectangle we get back doesn't account for the orientation of the screen, so we need to call the convertRect:fromView: method to switch the width and height if the device is in landscape mode.

Now that we have the ending keyboard height, we can calculate the new frame size for our text view. If the keyboard is appearing, we'll decrease the height of our text view by the height of the keyboard, and if the keyboard is disappearing, we'll increase the height of our text view by the height of the keyboard.

TextInput/Feelings6/Classes/FeelingsViewController.m

```
-(CGRect) adjustFrameHeightBy:(CGFloat) change
                 multipliedBy:(NSInteger) direction {
    return CGRectMake(20,
                      20,
                      self.textView.frame.size.width,
                      self.textView.frame.size.height + change * direction);
}
```

Use these helper methods to get the correct behavior in the keyboard-WillAppear: and keyboardWillDisappear: methods.

TextInput/Feelings6/Classes/FeelingsViewController.m

```
-(void)keyboardWillAppear:(NSNotification *)notification {
    [UIView beginAnimations:nil context:NULL];
    [self matchAnimationTo:[notification userInfo]];
```

```
    self.textView.frame =
        [self adjustFrameHeightBy:[self keyboardEndingFrameHeight:
                                                [notification userInfo]]
                    multipliedBy:-1];
    [UIView commitAnimations];
}
-(void)keyboardWillDisappear:(NSNotification *) notification {
    [UIView beginAnimations:nil context:NULL];
    [self matchAnimationTo:[notification userInfo]];
    self.textView.frame =
        [self adjustFrameHeightBy:[self keyboardEndingFrameHeight:
                                                [notification userInfo]]
                    multipliedBy:1];
    [UIView commitAnimations];
}
```

Build and run. Now the behavior is correct in both portrait and land-scape orientations. For example, when the keyboard is visible, the text view should look like this:

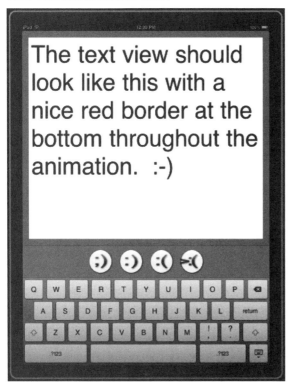

Check to see that you can rotate the device with the keyboard visible and dismiss the keyboard, and everything still animates properly. Creating custom keyboards and keyboard accessories is simple, but often there are details like these to take care of.

5.7 Summary

In this chapter, you saw how easy it is to provide your own custom keyboard, add an accessory to one of the keyboards Apple provides, or both. Remember, though, that you should have a clear need that a standard keyboard does not meet. Your users are going to be very familiar with the built-in keyboards. Make sure there's a compelling reason for using a nonstandard keyboard. Your custom keyboards add cognitive load. You need to be sure that they provide enough value to justify this effort.

For example, here is a custom keyboard from Apple's Numbers application:

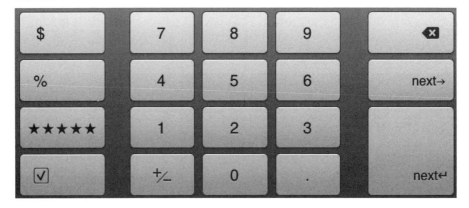

This nonstandard keyboard makes data entry for the selected cell faster and easier. Any time your user needs to enter text, you should first consider which of the standard keyboards to use, and then you should consider whether you can make their task easier by providing a custom keyboard. Remember, your goal is to make your app and the device disappear and allow your use to concentrate on what it is they are trying to experience or accomplish.

As you've seen in this chapter, you don't have to do very much to customize text input. You just need to set the inputView or inputAccessoryView property, configure it correctly, handle all appropriate actions, and make sure you move the elements around the keyboard properly.

Chapter 6

Custom Drawing

These new devices from Apple are keeping designers busy. You have a collection of images that you may have used in your iPhone app, and along comes the iPad. So, now you go back to the drawing board. An image that might look great on an iPhone might look too small on an iPad, so you may be creating iPhone and iPad versions of your images the way we did with icons in the very first chapter of this book.

The story doesn't end there. The iPhone 4 has a new display with twice the number of pixels in each direction. If you don't update your artwork to target this new device, you'll get that same fuzzy look that we got in the first chapter when we used the compatibility mode to run our iPhone apps on our iPad. So if you are targeting the iPhone and the iPad, you need three different versions of each image for these three different screens, and you know that there will be more before long.

We can ask our designers for three different versions of our digital assets, and in many cases this will be the right solution. Often, however, we can fairly easily draw some of the shapes that we need programmatically. It can be tedious, it can be a pain, but for simple examples it may be just the right choice.

In this chapter, we'll begin with the C-based APIs that have been around for years for drawing on the iPhone and the Mac. We'll then use the newly introduced Cocoa UIBezierPath class, which is almost the same as its Mac OS X cousin, the NSBezierPath class.

In either case, the general strategy for drawing is the same. You'll create a context and a path that you will either fill, stroke, or both. The details are often easier if you draw the object centered at (0,0) and later move it to wherever you want it to appear on the screen.

We'll begin this chapter with the C-based version of drawing a yellow triangle in the center of the screen. We'll then transform the example to a more familiar Cocoa setting and add more components to our drawing. We'll add ovals and rectangles and arcs of circles. Finally, we'll work with two forms of bezier curves and write the result out as a PDF.[1]

Even with the new and improved classes and methods introduced for the iPad, drawing in code is still pretty tedious. For a simple example like the one in this chapter, you might be better off creating three versions of a PNG in Photoshop or Omnigraffle and using them in your application. The point of the example isn't the end result but rather the techniques you'll learn along the way.

6.1 Drawing with Core Graphics

Create a new iPad view–based project named Bezier. Add a new subclass of UIView, and name it BezierView. Don't forget to change the type of your UIView in the BezierViewController nib to BezierView.

We'll do all of our drawing in the BezierView class. We could put all of our drawing code in the drawRect: method, but we'll follow good coding practices and break out much of the actual work into other methods. The drawRect: method outlines the work that needs to be done.

`Drawing/Bezier1/Classes/BezierView.m`

```
- (void)drawRect:(CGRect)rect {
    CGMutablePathRef triangle  = [self triangle];
    CGContextRef ctx = UIGraphicsGetCurrentContext();
    [self centerContext:ctx];
    [self fill:triangle
     withColor:[UIColor yellowColor]
     inContext:ctx];
    [self stroke:triangle
        withColor:[UIColor blackColor]
            width:20.0
        inContext:ctx];
    [self restoreContext:ctx];
    CGPathRelease(triangle);
}
```

---

1. You'll find a wealth of information on this topic in *Programming with Quartz, 2D, and PDF Graphics in Mac OS X* [GL06] and *Quartz 2D Graphics for Mac OS X Developers* [Tho06].

When we're done, we want to see something that looks like this:

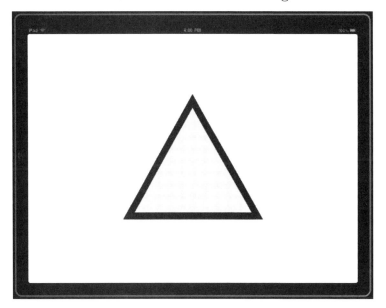

You can see that first we'll create a path for the triangle, and we'll get and save the current graphics context. CGMutablePath and CGContext are the fundamental objects used throughout the drawing process.

We create the triangle, move it to the center of the screen, fill it with yellow, stroke the boundary with a 20-pixel-wide black line, and then clean up after ourselves.

Let's explore each step.

Creating the Triangular Path

We create and hold on to our triangular path with this call from the drawRect: method:

```
CGMutablePathRef triangle  = [self triangle];
```

The method triangle creates a new mutable path and starts by moving it to the vertex at the top of the triangle. Then a line is added to the path (which is why it had to be mutable) down the right side of the triangle; then another is added across the bottom. In the end, a line is created to close off the triangle.

Drawing/Bezier1/Classes/BezierView.m

```
- (CGMutablePathRef) triangle {
    CGMutablePathRef path = CGPathCreateMutable();
    CGPathMoveToPoint(path, NULL, 0,-173);
```

```
          CGPathAddLineToPoint(path, NULL, 200,173);
          CGPathAddLineToPoint(path, NULL,-200,173);
          CGPathCloseSubpath(path);
          return path;
}
```

All of these operations are accomplished with C function calls. Note that the CGPathMoveToPoint(), CGPathAddLineToPoint(), and CGPathClose-Subpath() functions all take path as a parameter.

Moving the Path Here and Back

It's easier if you draw the path centered at (0,0) and move it later. This makes the calculations for your path easier, and it makes it relatively easy for you to reuse your work. For example, we could easily have created an app that stamps the yellow triangle wherever the user touches the screen. We would keep drawing triangles and moving them to wherever the touch is located.

The call to move the curve is contained in the following line in the drawRect: method:

```
[self centerContext:ctx];
```

There is a corresponding call to restoreContext: after the drawing is done to clean things back up. There's not much to those two methods:

Drawing/Bezier1/Classes/BezierView.m
```
-(void) centerContext:(CGContextRef) ctx {
    CGPoint center = [self convertPoint:self.center fromView:nil];
    CGContextSaveGState(ctx);
    CGContextTranslateCTM(ctx, center.x, center.y);
}
-(void) restoreContext:(CGContextRef) ctx {
    CGContextRestoreGState(ctx);
}
```

In centerContext:, we calculate the center of view, allowing for device rotation. Before we move the context, we store the current Core Graphics state. We then translate the context to the center of the view. This means the triangle is now centered at the center of the view and not in the top-left corner. After the drawing is done, we restore the state to the value we preserved.

Stroking and Filling

At this point, we've done most of the work. We've created the triangle and moved it to the center of the screen. Unfortunately, there's nothing to see yet. We'll add color with these calls from the drawRect: method:

```
[self fill:triangle
 withColor:[UIColor yellowColor]
 inContext:ctx];
[self stroke:triangle
    withColor:[UIColor blackColor]
        width:20.0
    inContext:ctx];
```

It's not surprising that you have to pass the path into these methods that will be stroking and filling the triangle. It is, however, a bit surprising that you have to pass in the context. When you look at the implementation of these methods, you'll see that the context is needed as a parameter for each one of the function calls.

Drawing/Bezier1/Classes/BezierView.m

```
- (void) fill: (CGMutablePathRef) path
    withColor:(UIColor *) color
    inContext: (CGContextRef) ctx  {
    CGContextSetFillColorWithColor(ctx, color.CGColor);
    CGContextAddPath(ctx, path);
    CGContextFillPath(ctx);
}
- (void) stroke:(CGMutablePathRef) path
     withColor:(UIColor *) color
         width:(CGFloat) width
      inContext:(CGContextRef) ctx {
    CGContextSetStrokeColorWithColor(ctx, color.CGColor);
    CGContextSetLineWidth(ctx, width);
    CGContextAddPath(ctx, path);
    CGContextStrokePath(ctx);
}
```

In each case, we set the color to be used, add the path to this modified context, and then either stroke or fill the path. Finally, there's something to see. You should see a big yellow triangle with a thick black border in the center of your screen.

In the next section, we'll rework this example using the UIBezierPath class. There is no real reason for doing so. The UIBezierPath class has more features that make it quite attractive, but if you are just building paths out of line segments and simple curves, you can use the C-based APIs described in this section.

6.2 Using the Cocoa APIs

You can see right away in the drawRect: method that our implementation is simpler in the Cocoa version. Most striking, we have not explicitly used the graphics context. We didn't have to get a reference to it and pass it in to the methods that fill and stroke the triangle.

Drawing/Bezier2/Classes/BezierView.m

```
- (void)drawRect:(CGRect)rect {
    UIBezierPath *triangle = [[self triangle] retain];
    [self centerPath: triangle];
    [self fill:triangle withColor:[UIColor yellowColor]];
    [self stroke:triangle withColor:[UIColor blackColor] width:20.0];
    [triangle release];
}
```

Now that we have a Cocoa implementation, we have to follow the reference-counting rules in that setting, so we need to add a retain to hang on to our triangle while we are moving and drawing it. Let's look at the rest of the differences in this implementation at each stage.

Creating the Triangular Path

The translation from the C functions to the Objective-C method calls is pretty straightforward. For example, this:

```
CGPathMoveToPoint(path, NULL, 0,-173);
```

becomes the following:

```
[path moveToPoint:CGPointMake(0,-173)];
```

You don't have to pass in the path variable as a parameter as you are sending the message to it. Make similar changes throughout to get the Cocoa version of the triangle method.

Drawing/Bezier2/Classes/BezierView.m

```
- (UIBezierPath *) triangle {
    UIBezierPath *path = [UIBezierPath bezierPath];
    [path moveToPoint:CGPointMake(0,-173)];
    [path addLineToPoint:CGPointMake(200,173)];
    [path addLineToPoint:CGPointMake(-200,173)];
    [path closePath];
    return path;
}
```

Each method is little more than a thin wrapper on top of a C function, and yet this approach feels cleaner. That, of course, is in the eye of the beholder, which is why we present both versions for you.[2]

Moving the Path

This time we move the path and not the context:

Drawing/Bezier2/Classes/BezierView.m

```
-(void) centerPath:(UIBezierPath *) path {
    CGPoint center = [self convertPoint:self.center fromView:nil];
    [path applyTransform:CGAffineTransformMakeTranslation(center.x, center.y)];
}
```

As before, we calculate the center, but this time we apply the transform to the path. In this case, we use a simple translation to move the center of the triangle to the center of the view.

Before, we needed to restore the context. Here we don't do that. Here if we are going to place several triangles at different locations, we would have to make a copy of the triangle and move, fill, and stroke it. We'd make a change like this to the drawRect: method:

```
- (void)drawRect:(CGRect)rect {
►    UIBezierPath *triangleTemplate  = [self triangle];
►    UIBezierPath *triangle = [triangleTemplate copy];
    [self centerPath: triangle];
    [self fill:triangle withColor:[UIColor yellowColor]];
    [self stroke:triangle withColor:[UIColor blackColor] width:20.0];
►    [triangle release];
►    [triangleTemplate release];
}
```

Stroking and Filling

We don't have to explicitly use the context when setting the colors or when stroking and filling. The current context is stored and restored on either side of a call to stroke or fill.

Drawing/Bezier2/Classes/BezierView.m

```
- (void) fill: (UIBezierPath *) path
    withColor:(UIColor *) color   {
    [color setFill];
    [path fill];
}
```

---

2. You can actually mix the two approaches, but there are problems with keeping the information in sync in the two worlds. If you want to mix the C and Cocoa APIs, you should read the "Graphics" section in Apple's *iPad Programming Guide* [App10b].

```
- (void) stroke:(UIBezierPath *) path
       withColor:(UIColor *) color
           width:(CGFloat) width  {
    [color setStroke];
    path.lineWidth = width;
    [path stroke];
}
```

Many people have problems with this step. It is easy to see why you send the fill message to the path, but the way in which we set the stroke and fill colors seems odd. Here we send a color a message that it is the stroke color or the fill color. It's as if we say, "Yellow crayon, get ready to do the filling." Then we say, "Let the filling begin," and the yellow crayon knows that that is its job.

Shouldn't the stroke and fill colors be properties on the UIBezierPath instance? Probably. They're not. This is the way you need to do it.

If this were all there were to UIBezierPaths, you might ask, "What's the big deal?" Fortunately, we can use them to draw rectangles, circles, rounded rectangles, and, as you might have guessed, bezier curves. We look at that next.

6.3 Drawing Circles and Rectangles

Let's add an exclamation point to the middle of the triangle. Our exclamation point will start out as a rectangle for the top and a dot for the bottom.

In the drawRect:, you just need to add the following highlighted lines to create the exclamation point, move it, and fill it with black:

Drawing/Bezier3/Classes/BezierView.m

```
- (void)drawRect:(CGRect)rect {
    UIBezierPath *triangle = [[self triangle] retain];
    [self centerPath: triangle];
    [self fill:triangle withColor:[UIColor yellowColor]];
    [self stroke:triangle withColor:[UIColor blackColor] width:20.0];
```

```
▶       UIBezierPath *exclamationPoint = [[self exclamationPoint] retain];
▶       [self centerPath:exclamationPoint];
▶       [self fill:exclamationPoint withColor:[UIColor blackColor]];
▶       [exclamationPoint release];
        [triangle release];
    }
```

The exclamation point consists of two pieces: the top and the dot at the bottom. Use the appendPath: to build the exclamation point out of these two components:

Drawing/Bezier3/Classes/BezierView.m

```
- (UIBezierPath *) exclamationPoint {
    UIBezierPath *path = [UIBezierPath bezierPath];
    [path appendPath:[self top]];
    [path appendPath:[self dot]];
    return path;
}
```

The top is a rectangle created with the bezierPathWithRect: method, and the bottom is a circle made with the bezierPathWithOvalInRect:.

Drawing/Bezier3/Classes/BezierView.m

```
- (UIBezierPath *) top {
    return [UIBezierPath
            bezierPathWithRect:CGRectMake(-20, -70, 40, 140)];
}
- (UIBezierPath *) dot {
    return [UIBezierPath
            bezierPathWithOvalInRect:CGRectMake(-25, 95, 50, 50)];
}
```

From here to the end of the chapter we'll make little changes to the top to change the look of the exclamation point. For example, we can soften the corners a bit by changing the rectangle to a rounded rectangle:

Drawing/Bezier4/Classes/BezierView.m

```
- (UIBezierPath *) top {
    return [UIBezierPath
            bezierPathWithRoundedRect:CGRectMake(-20, -70, 40, 140)
                        cornerRadius:8.0];
}
```

We can round the corners even more using a corner radius equal to half the width of the rectangle:

Drawing/Bezier5/Classes/BezierView.m

```
- (UIBezierPath *) top {
    return [UIBezierPath
            bezierPathWithRoundedRect:CGRectMake(-20, -70, 40, 140)
                          cornerRadius:20.0];
}
```

This looks as if we've placed a semicircle at both ends of the rectangle:

Next, we'll modify the path and add arcs from circles to the paths.

6.4 Irregular Paths

We'll modify the path for the top portion of the exclamation point so that it tapers at the bottom. The main purpose is to ensure that it is not built from a rectangle:

Drawing/Bezier6/Classes/BezierView.m

```
- (UIBezierPath *) top {
    UIBezierPath *path = [UIBezierPath bezierPath];
    [path moveToPoint:CGPointMake(-30, -70)];
    [path addLineToPoint:CGPointMake(30, -70)];
    [path addLineToPoint:CGPointMake(5, 70)];
    [path addLineToPoint:CGPointMake(-5, 70)];
    [path closePath];
    return path;
}
```

You've seen how to build up paths from other paths and how to build the paths from lines and curves. The component parts are simple, but the combination can be powerful and complex. For example, make the following highlighted changes to replace the line segments on the top and the bottom of the top portion of the exclamation points with half circles.

Drawing/Bezier7/Classes/BezierView.m

```
- (UIBezierPath *) top {
    UIBezierPath *path = [UIBezierPath bezierPath];
    [path moveToPoint:CGPointMake(-30, -70)];
    [path appendPath:[UIBezierPath bezierPathWithArcCenter:CGPointMake(0, -70)
                                                    radius:30
                                                startAngle:M_PI
                                                  endAngle:2*M_PI
                                                 clockwise:YES]];
    [path addLineToPoint:CGPointMake(30, -70)];
    [path addLineToPoint:CGPointMake(5, 70)];
    [path appendPath:[UIBezierPath bezierPathWithArcCenter:CGPointMake(0, 70)
                                                    radius:5
                                                startAngle:0
                                                  endAngle:M_PI
                                                 clockwise:YES]];
    [path addLineToPoint:CGPointMake(-30, -70)];
    return path;
}
```

For each circular arc, we specify the center and radius of the circle and the beginning and end angles in radians. We also need to indicate whether you are traveling clockwise or counterclockwise from start to finish. In our case, we are traversing each arc clockwise. This is only partly because we are traveling clockwise around the path. If we traversed the arcs counterclockwise, we would have dips instead of bumps at the end.

If you traveled the path in the opposite direction, you would have to also follow each arc counterclockwise to make sure that you have the bumps instead of dips.

Although the curves look as if they fit the shape smoothly, they do not. There is a very slight corner at each of the four points where the straight-line segments meet the circular arcs. In our case, these corners are undetectable, so we could ignore them. Remember, though, that the purpose of this chapter is to introduce you to useful techniques. It's time to meet the methods that the UIBezierPath class is named for.

6.5 Using Bezier Curves

The UIBezierPath class allows you to draw two types of bezier curves. The quadratic curve is specified by two endpoints and a single control point that defines the tangent directions at each endpoint.

In code we use the addQuadCurveToPoint:controlPoint: method. We specify only two points: the ending point and the control point. The starting point is equal to the current value of the path's currentPoint property. The resulting curve is a quadratic that starts at the currentPoint with initial direction equal to the vector defined by the currentPoint and the control point. The curve ends at the ending point, which is passed in as the first parameter to the method with a final direction equal to the vector defined by the control point and this ending point.

Here we replace the bottom arc with a quadratic bezier curve:

Drawing/Bezier8/Classes/BezierView.m

```
- (UIBezierPath *) top {
    UIBezierPath *path = [UIBezierPath bezierPath];
    [path moveToPoint:CGPointMake(-30, -70)];
    [path appendPath:[UIBezierPath bezierPathWithArcCenter:CGPointMake(0, -70)
                                                    radius:30
                                                startAngle:M_PI
                                                  endAngle:2*M_PI
                                                 clockwise:YES]];
    [path addLineToPoint:CGPointMake(30, -70)];
    [path addLineToPoint:CGPointMake(5, 70)];
▶   [path addQuadCurveToPoint:CGPointMake(-5, 70)
▶              controlPoint:CGPointMake(0, 98)];
    [path addLineToPoint:CGPointMake(-30, -70)];
    return path;
}
```

The control point was chosen to be the point at which the two sides of the exclamation point would meet if they were extended.

We can't use that trick for the top curve of the exclamation point because the two sides are diverging at that point. In fact, we could not cap the curve with a quadratic without introducing corners at the two join points. We'll use a cubic bezier curve because that uses two control points: one to set the curve's tangent direction at each endpoint.[3]

Drawing/Bezier9/Classes/BezierView.m

```
- (UIBezierPath *) top {
    UIBezierPath *path = [UIBezierPath bezierPath];
    [path moveToPoint:CGPointMake(-30, -70)];
▶   [path addCurveToPoint:CGPointMake(30, -70)
▶           controlPoint1:CGPointMake(-35, -98)
▶           controlPoint2:CGPointMake(35, -98)];
    [path addLineToPoint:CGPointMake(30, -70)];
    [path addLineToPoint:CGPointMake(5, 70)];
    [path addQuadCurveToPoint:CGPointMake(-5, 70)
               controlPoint:CGPointMake(0, 98)];
    [path addLineToPoint:CGPointMake(-30, -70)];
    return path;
}
```

The starting point is again the path's currentPoint, and the initial direction is set by currentPoint and the first control point. The ending point is again the method's first parameter, and the ending direction is set

---

3. You'll find illustrations of both types of bezier curves and how their endpoints and control points are used in Apple's *iPad Programming Guide* [App10b].

by the second control point and this ending point. The result is a curve that smoothly joins each of the sides.

Let's move the control points out a bit further:

Drawing/Bezier10/Classes/BezierView.m

```
[path addCurveToPoint:CGPointMake(30, -70)
        controlPoint1:CGPointMake(-40, -126)
        controlPoint2:CGPointMake(40, -126)];
```

You can see that the length of the vectors describing the direction also changes the bezier curve:

You can experiment with the control points and the sides of the exclamation point until you have exactly the look that you want.

6.6 Saving Our Drawing as a PDF

Let's extract the contents of the drawRect: method so that we can use the same drawing commands to draw to the screen and to produce a PDF of the image:

Drawing/Bezier11/Classes/BezierView.m

```
-(void) drawInCurrentContext {
    UIBezierPath *triangle = [[self triangle] retain];
    [self centerPath: triangle];
    [self fill:triangle withColor:[UIColor yellowColor]];
    [self stroke:triangle withColor:[UIColor blackColor] width:20.0];
    UIBezierPath *exclamationPoint = [[self exclamationPoint] retain];
    [self centerPath:exclamationPoint];
    [self fill:exclamationPoint withColor:[UIColor blackColor]];
```

```
    [exclamationPoint release];
    [triangle release];
}
- (void)drawRect:(CGRect)rect {
    [self drawInCurrentContext];
}
```

If we build and run, we get the same results as before, but we can now set the PDF context and call drawInCurrentContext to draw our warning shape to a PDF file in the Documents directory. As a first step, the pathToWarningFile returns our path where we'll create and save our PDF using the applicationDocumentDirectory method.

Drawing/Bezier12/Classes/BezierView.m

```
- (NSString *)applicationDocumentsDirectory {
      return [NSSearchPathForDirectoriesInDomains(NSDocumentDirectory,
                                     NSUserDomainMask, YES)
                                          lastObject];
}
-(NSString *) pathToWarningFile {
    return [[self applicationDocumentsDirectory]
                      stringByAppendingPathComponent:@"Warning.pdf"];
}
```

This gives us the path to the Warning.pdf file in the Documents directory. We'll pass that in as the first parameter to the UIGraphicsBeginPDFContextToFile() function that we use to create and configure the current context to be used for creating a PDF that will be saved to file. The other two parameters are the page size as a CGRect and an optional NSDictionary containing document information. We're using the view's dimensions as the dimensions of the page. You can use CGRectMake() to create a CGRect or use CGRectZero() to create a page that is 8.5 by 11 inches or 612 by 792 pixels.

Instead of saving the PDF directly to a file, you could use the function UIGraphicsBeginPDFContextToData() to write the PDF to an NSData object. We'll write to a file.

You start by creating a new PDF page, and then you draw to the PDF page the same way you draw to the screen. We're just going to use the same page information throughout our document so we can use the UIGraphicsBeginPDFPage() method. You can change the page information when you create a new page by using the UIGraphicsBeginPDFPageWithInfo() function.

If you need another page, then you begin another one using one of those two functions. When you are done with your last page, you end the PDF context. In our simple example, we have only a single page. Here's the code to create the PDF:

```
Drawing/Bezier12/Classes/BezierView.m
```

```
- (void)drawRect:(CGRect)rect {
    [self drawInCurrentContext];
    UIGraphicsBeginPDFContextToFile([self pathToWarningFile],self.frame,nil);
    UIGraphicsBeginPDFPage();
    [self drawInCurrentContext];
    UIGraphicsEndPDFContext();
}
```

We used exactly the same code to write to the PDF that we did to write to the screen. The only difference is we begin by setting the context and creating a new page, and we end by closing the context. Build and run in the simulator. You can find the PDF you created by following the path to the applications: Library/Application\ Support/iPhone\ Simulator/3.2/Applications. You'll see a bunch of numbered directories. Look inside of each one until you find our application. Find the directory corresponding to the Bezier application, and look inside of its Documents directory. You should find the Warning.pdf file. It contains the warning symbol.

You can read more about writing to PDFs in Apple's *iPad Programming Guide* [App10b] in the "Graphics and Drawing" section.

6.7 Summary

The UIBezierPath class makes drawing easier and more powerful. You always have the opportunity to instead use a drawing program to generate an image file that you can use in your application. If the drawing code isn't overly complicated, then you should prefer to do your drawing in code rather than bring in such an image.[4]

---

4. You'll see a discussion of that in a blog post by Jeff LaMarche responding to a comment by Joe Conway. Start with this site: http://iphonedevelopment.blogspot.com/2010/05/some-good-advice.html.

Chapter 7

The Movie Player

At its core, the iPad is designed for media consumption; the large, in-hand screen is perfect for graphic display, especially video. With an iPhone, you can display video only in a full-screen viewer, while the iPad's SDK allows you to build video right into your applications and fully customize the user experience around it. The SDK also exposes the state of the player, so you can directly control the video and coordinate its playback with the rest of your application.

In the next two chapters, we're going to explore the movie player controller: embedding it in an application, overlaying other views on top of it, creating our own custom playback control and playlist, generating navigational thumbnails, and streaming content. If you've used video player frameworks in the past, you probably found them to be difficult to work with. With Apple's new framework, we'll have a sophisticated player running quickly.

7.1 Setting Up a View for the Movie

In the next few pages, we're going to get a video playing from scratch in an iPad application. Once we've done that, we're going to step back and look at the MPMoviePlayerController architecture in detail and make our implementation a lot more interesting. We've already prepared a project for you in the MoviePlayer1 folder (if you prefer to really start from scratch, you can create a view-based project). Open the project, and you'll find that we've added a video to the Resources directory called

Figure 7.1: SETTING UP THE MOVIE PLAYER VIEW

BigBuckBunny_640x360.m4v.[1] We've also added the MediaPlayer.framework to your frameworks folder.

We're going to first focus on getting an MPMoviePlayerController instantiated to manage the playback of our video. This class manages all the details of playback and gives you a view that you can add to your own view hierarchy to display video. The MPMoviePlayerController can also display our video content full-screen (we'll get to that later in the chapter).

Let's start by opening the MoviePlayerViewController.xib nib file in Interface Builder and adding a view that can be used to hold the MPMoviePlay-

---

1. Depending on your distribution, you may actually need to download this movie (and add it to your project), which you can find at http://www.bigbuckbunny.org. Note that this movie is copyright Blender Foundation, http://www.bigbuckbunny.org.

erController's video.[2] Begin by selecting the MoviePlayerViewController's main view and resetting its background color to solid black. Then drag a UIView object from the Interface Builder Library into the view. You'll want to use the Size inspector to configure your new UIView, as we've done in Figure 7.1, on the facing page. Make sure to copy the size and autosizing constraints in your version.

Now we need to create an outlet to this new view in our MoviePlayerView-Controller header file, like this:

`movieplayer/MoviePlayer1/Classes/MoviePlayerViewController.h`

```
@interface MoviePlayerViewController : UIViewController {
        UIView *viewForMovie;
}

@property (nonatomic, retain) IBOutlet UIView *viewForMovie;
@end
```

Here we've defined an UIView named viewForMovie and also declared it as a property that is an IBOutlet. Don't forget to also add the synthesize directive to the MoviePlayer1ViewController.m file:

`movieplayer/MoviePlayer1/Classes/MoviePlayerViewController.m`

```
@synthesize viewForMovie;
```

Now let's wire things up by going back to the MoviePlayerViewController.xib nib file in Interface Builder. We're going to connect the IBOutlet (for view-ForMovie) that we just declared to the UIView. To do that, Control+click the nib file's File's Owner object, and drag to the new view. When the connection popup appears, choose viewForMovie, as we've done in Figure 7.2, on the next page.

Meet the MPMoviePlayerController

With the Interface Builder work out of the way, let's focus on code. We're going to add an instance of the MPMoviePlayerController class by declaring it in the MoviePlayerViewController.h header file. First we need to import the movie player's MPMoviePlayerController.h file and then add a declaration for the player; we'll also declare the player as a property. While we're here, let's also add a declaration for a method named movieURL (we'll come back to this shortly).

---

2. Just to make sure we have this straight, the MoviePlayerViewController is the main view controller that we are writing for our application; the MPMoviePlayerController is a class that is part of iOS 3.2, written by Apple, and manages video playback.

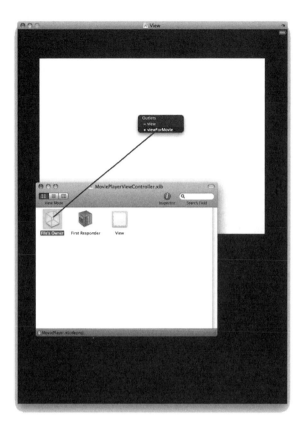

Figure 7.2: WIRING UP THE MOVIE VIEW

movieplayer/MoviePlayer1/Classes/MoviePlayerViewController.h

```
#import <UIKit/UIKit.h>
#import <MediaPlayer/MPMoviePlayerController.h>


@interface MoviePlayerViewController : UIViewController {
        UIView *viewForMovie;
        MPMoviePlayerController *player;
}

@property (nonatomic, retain) IBOutlet UIView *viewForMovie;
@property (nonatomic, retain) MPMoviePlayerController *player;

-(NSURL *)movieURL;
@end
```

Let's take a look at the MoviePlayerViewController.m implementation file. We start in the viewDidLoad: method and instantiate the MPMoviePlayerController there. Let's add the code and then walk through it:

movieplayer/MoviePlayer1/Classes/MoviePlayerViewController.m

```
- (void)viewDidLoad {
        [super viewDidLoad];

        self.player = [[MPMoviePlayerController alloc] init];
        self.player.contentURL = [self movieURL];
}
```

Here, we've first alloc'd and init'd the movie controller and assigned it to our player property. Next we assigned a content URL to the player—this is the location of the video content we want the player to play back, which can be a local file in the bundle or a network-based URL. For now, we're going to use a local file for our video content. Let's take a quick detour to look at the movieURL method that constructs a file-based URL to the video content in the bundle:

movieplayer/MoviePlayer1/Classes/MoviePlayerViewController.m

```
-(NSURL *)movieURL
{
        NSBundle *bundle = [NSBundle mainBundle];
        NSString *moviePath =
        [bundle
         pathForResource:@"BigBuckBunny_640x360"
         ofType:@"m4v"];
        if (moviePath) {
                return [NSURL fileURLWithPath:moviePath];
        } else {
                return nil;
        }
}
```

If you've ever constructed a URL to an image or other resource in the bundle, this code should look familiar: here we obtain a reference to the bundle, then construct a URL to our movie, wrap it in an NSURL object, and return it. We'll come back to this code later in the chapter and construct some network-based URLs to stream content to the iPad.

Back from our detour, we're now going to look at one of the most important concepts in this chapter: the use of the MPMoviePlayerController's video property. As we mentioned earlier, the player controller maintains a special view that can be added as a subview to any of your views to display video content. Treat this view with kid gloves—although we'll find some interesting reasons to add our own subviews to the player's view later in the chapter, in general this is an opaque object under the control of the player and should be treated that way.

movieplayer/MoviePlayer1/Classes/MoviePlayerViewController.m

```
- (void)viewDidLoad {
        [super viewDidLoad];

        self.player = [[MPMoviePlayerController alloc] init];
        self.player.contentURL = [self movieURL];

▶       self.player.view.frame = self.viewForMovie.bounds;
▶       self.player.view.autoresizingMask =
▶               UIViewAutoresizingFlexibleWidth |
▶               UIViewAutoresizingFlexibleHeight;
▶
▶       [self.viewForMovie addSubview:player.view];
▶       [self.player play];

}
```

Getting access to the MPMoviePlayerController's video view is easy; we just access the player's view property like any other property, and that's what we're doing in this code. After we have a reference to the view, we're first setting two properties: the view's frame and a couple of masks that control how the view can be resized. The frame, like the frame of any view, controls its on-screen size. Here, we're getting the frame from the movieForView object and mirroring that. For the masks, we're setting the view so that if necessary, it can be resized by width or height.

Now for the interesting part: we're taking the player controller's view and adding it as a subview to the viewForMovie view that we created earlier in Interface Builder. With that done, we send the player the play message to start the show. At this point, build and run your project, and you should see video playing in your UIView. Touching the view should expose some controls, including a full-screen control, and rotating the device should give you reasonable resizing behavior.

The Big Picture, or What Just Happened?

Let's think about what just happened—it can get a bit confusing the first time through. Although this may seem a bit complex, once you get past all the views and controllers involved, it is actually fairly simple.

What we've done is create an MPMoviePlayerController object that acts as the controller for displaying video content. We'll get into the specifics shortly, but we can use this controller to manage all the aspects of video playback, including stop, start, pause, and other actions. This controller also exposes a built-in property, called view, that we can obtain a reference to and then add to our own views to display video. And that's exactly what we did. Remember, we first created an UIView in Interface Builder to act as a landing place for the video view; then, after creating the MPMoviePlayerController, we took its internal view and added it as a subview to our UIView. The result? Video playback right in our application.

7.2 Peeking into the Player

Now that we have a player instantiated with its view attached to our view hierarchy, let's get a little information from the player about the video and what it's doing. To do that, we're going to add an info button and a label to the movie player application and then use the MPMoviePlayerController to display some real-time information in the label when the button is touched.

Let's get the mechanics out of the way before we dive into the MPMoviePlayerController code—reopen the MoviePlayerViewController.xib nib file in Interface Builder, and drag a UILabel view and a UIButton view onto the main view. Position both at the bottom of the iPad screen, as in Figure 7.3, on the following page.

We also want to do a few things to properly configure the label and the button. First, set the label text to be white, and remove the default label text. Then set its autosizing to stay positioned relative to the bottom of the screen. Then we need to change the style of the button to Info Light, rather than the default of Rounded Rect, and set its autosizing as we did with the label.

Now we're going to create an action for the info button, called getInfo, and an outlet for the label, called onScreenDisplayLabel. Let's do that by first making the additions to the MoviePlayerViewController.h header file:

movieplayer/MoviePlayer2/Classes/MoviePlayerViewController.h

```
@interface MoviePlayerViewController : UIViewController {
        UIView *viewForMovie;
        MPMoviePlayerController *player;
►       UILabel *onScreenDisplayLabel:
}

@property (nonatomic, retain) IBOutlet UIView *viewForMovie;
@property (nonatomic, retain) MPMoviePlayerController *player;
► @property (nonatomic, retain) IBOutlet UILabel *onScreenDisplayLabel;

 - (NSURL *)movieURL;
► - (IBAction)getInfo:(id)sender;
@end
```

Figure 7.3: PLACING THE LABEL AND BUTTON VIEWS AND CONFIGURING THE LABEL

Now that you've updated the MoviePlayerViewController.h header file, return to Interface Builder, and connect the onScreenDisplayLabel IBOutlet to the label; then set the action of the info button to the getInfo: method.

Now we're ready to dive into the MPMoviePlayerController. Because it's responsible for managing the playback, the MPMoviePlayerController maintains a set of properties describing the current video asset, as well as runtime information about the video's size, duration, and current playback position (to name a few). We'll touch on many of these properties in this chapter, but for an exhaustive list, as well as more details about their semantics, refer to the *MPMoviePlayerController Class Reference* [App10c].

Let's use a few of these properties to write our getInf:o method:

`movieplayer/MoviePlayer2/Classes/MoviePlayerViewController.m`

```
- (void) getInfo:(id)sender
{
        MPMoviePlayerController *moviePlayer = self.player;

        float width = moviePlayer.naturalSize.width;
        float height = moviePlayer.naturalSize.height;
        float playbackTime = moviePlayer.currentPlaybackTime;
        float playbackRate = moviePlayer.currentPlaybackRate;
        float duration = moviePlayer.duration;

        onScreenDisplayLabel.text =
                [NSString stringWithFormat:
                        @"[Time: %.1f of %.f secs] \
                         [Playback: %.0fx] \
                         [Size: %.0fx%.0f]",
                                playbackTime,
                                duration,
                                playbackRate,
                                width,
                                height];
}
```

Here we're getting a reference to the movie controller and then using its naturalSize property to get the actual size of the video asset playing. Note that the player might be scaling the video to fit within another frame size (if this is important to your application, you can examine the player's frame, as well as its scalingMode properties), but this property gives you the true, native size of the video.

We're then looking at three properties related to the video's playback: the current playback time within the video (currentPlaybackTime), the total duration of the video (duration), and the playback rate (currentPlaybackRate). While the duration is a readonly property, the other two properties can be set to affect the current play position and the playback rate, respectively. They're also part of the MPMediaPlayback protocol, which the MPMoviePlayerController class implements and give us a standardized interface for playing back media (with common methods such as play, pause, start, stop, and seek). We'll get back to these methods later in this chapter and in the next.

Compile and run this new code. Touch the info button; in fact, touch it as many times as you like, and you'll see the current state of these properties update as you do. When you touch the info button, you'll see something like this:

```
[Time: 1.5 of 596 secs] [Playback: 1x] [Size: 640x359]
```

Now that we've written this code, we have to come clean and tell you there's a point we've been glossing over: many of these properties aren't known until the video reaches some level of loading in the controller. In our current situation, the controller is loading from a local file, so this happens very quickly, but we could be retrieving the asset over the network—which would introduce a lot of delay. In fact, it would be quite easy to touch the info button long before these properties are known. So, how do we know then the player's properties are ready? That's what we're going to look at now, by introducing how the player communicates its state to an application through notifications.

7.3 Being Notified

The MPMoviePlayerController class supports a rich set of notifications that you can use to keep informed about the state of movie playback. As you might expect, you can be notified for playback events, such as stop, start, pause, and end events, but you can also receive notifications for the following:

- The availability of metadata about the video
- Changes to scaling and video resolution (including changes to and from full-screen mode)
- Changes to state based on the loading of network-based video
- The availability of generated thumbnails (we'll come back to this later)

We won't cover these all in detail, but we will work through the mechanics of using the MPMoviePlayerController classes' notifications and also work with the thumbnail capability in a later section.

For now, let's return to the problem of accessing properties (such as the video's duration) before the player has loaded enough of the video to have that information. Using notifications, we can solve this problem by registering to receive a notification when metadata is available. Here are the metadata-based notifications we can receive:

- MPMovieDurationAvailableNotification: Sent when the video duration has been determined
- MPMovieMediaTypesAvailableNotification: Sent when the audio and or video types have been determined
- MPMovieNaturalSizeAvailableNotification: Sent when the width and height of the video are known

Let's write some code to use the MPMovieDurationAvailableNotification notification; as a simple test, we'll call our getInfo action directly when the duration becomes available (we're also assuming that when the duration is available, other metadata is too; most likely this is a safe assumption, but obviously you want to check values for validity). Note that a better implementation might set the info button to disabled and then, when the metadata is available, enable it. For now, though, we're working through the mechanics of using notifications with the MPMoviePlayerController—we're going to return to a more complex example of notification in the next section.

Digging into Notifications

The movie player controller uses Cocoa's standard notification system. Here's a quick refresher: to receive notifications, you add an object as an observer to a named notification (such as MPMovieDurationAvailableNotification) and supply a selector that is called whenever there is a notification. You can also supply an optional payload object that is passed along to the observer upon each notification; if a payload object isn't supplied (by using a value of nil), the object sending the notification is passed along.

Here's the code to register your MoviePlayerViewController to receive the MPMovieDurationAvailableNotification notification; we're going to place this new code in the viewDidLoad method so that it is registered before the movie player is instantiated. We're setting movieDurationAvailable: as the selector for the notification, so any time an MPMovieDurationAvailableNotification is sent, this method will be called.

`movieplayer/MoviePlayer3/Classes/MoviePlayerViewController.m`

```
- (void)viewDidLoad {
        [super viewDidLoad];

        [[NSNotificationCenter defaultCenter]
                addObserver:self
                selector:@selector(movieDurationAvailable:)
                name:MPMovieDurationAvailableNotification
                object:nil];

        self.player = [[MPMoviePlayerController alloc] init];
        self.player.contentURL = [self movieURL];

        self.player.view.frame = self.viewForMovie.bounds;
        self.player.view.autoresizingMask =
                UIViewAutoresizingFlexibleWidth |
                UIViewAutoresizingFlexibleHeight;
```

```
        [self.viewForMovie addSubview:player.view];
        [self.player play];
}
```

That's all there is to setting up the notification on the movie player; now we just need to write the method that is called when a notification arrives:

movieplayer/MoviePlayer3/Classes/MoviePlayerViewController.m

```
- (void) movieDurationAvailable:(NSNotification*)notification {
        [self getInfo:nil];
}
```

All we're doing in this method is calling the getInfo method, so when you build and run this code, as soon as the duration is available, you should see the label populated, just as if you touched the info button. A more conventional use of this notification would be to obtain the duration directly in the method. How would we do that? Like this:

```
MPMoviePlayerController *moviePlayer = [notification object];
float duration = [moviePlayer duration];
```

Here we first obtain the player object from the notification (remember, we didn't supply a payload object, so instead the object sending the notification—in other words, the movie player—is passed to us), and then we can directly obtain the value using the duration property. Although technically we could have just accessed self.player.duration, more generally we may have placed the movieDurationAvailable: method in any arbitrary object that doesn't have direct access to the player, so the notification object gives us a way to access the player in a more uncoupled manner.

Now that we have simple notifications under our belt, let's move on to a much more interesting example.

7.4 Adding a Playlist

Now that we know how to receive notifications from the player, we're going to use them to write a simple playlist handler for our player. Note that we're not talking about the iTunes playlists; you can access them, and you'll want to look at the framework to do that. Here we're going to write a playlist controller to handle playlists of your own video media.

To do this, we're going to keep things simple and use an array to represent the model for our playlist (in a real application, you'll usually retrieve the playlist from the cloud). Let's create a PlaylistController to get started: to do that in Xcode, create a subclass of a table view controller named PlaylistController.m. Open the associated PlaylistController.h, and add these properties:

movieplayer/MoviePlayer3withPlaylist/Classes/PlaylistController.h

```
@interface PlaylistController : UITableViewController {
        NSArray *items;
        MoviePlayerViewController *playerController;
}
```

We're going to use the items array to hold a dictionary per playlist item, which will hold the title of the playlist item, along with its file-name. We're going to use the player property to hold a reference to our MPMoviePlayerController. Let's get the player property set up now by defining an init method for the PlaylistController class:

movieplayer/MoviePlayer3withPlaylist/Classes/PlaylistController.m

```
-(id)initWithPlayer:(MoviePlayerViewController *)thePlayer {
        self = [super init];
        if (self) {
                playerController = thePlayer;
        }
        return self;
}
```

Here we take the player and assign it to the local property—we'll alter the MovePlayerViewController in a bit to instantiate this class and pass it the active movie player. For now, let's keep working on the playlist controller by actually creating a list of items for the playlist using our items array. To do that, let's set this up in the viewDidLoad method:

movieplayer/MoviePlayer3withPlaylist/Classes/PlaylistController.m

```
- (void)viewDidLoad {
        [super viewDidLoad];

        items = [[NSArray arrayWithObjects:
                [NSDictionary dictionaryWithObjectsAndKeys:
                 @"Introduction", @"title",
                 [playerController
                  movieURL:@"elephantsdream-720-h264-st-aac-1"
                  withFiletype:@"mov"], @"URL",
                 nil],
                [NSDictionary dictionaryWithObjectsAndKeys:
                 @"Watch out!", @"title",
                 [playerController
                  movieURL:@"elephantsdream-720-h264-st-aac-2"
                  withFiletype:@"mov"], @"URL",
                 nil],
```

```
                        [NSDictionary dictionaryWithObjectsAndKeys:
                         @"Follow me!", @"title",
                         [playerController
                          movieURL:@"elephantsdream-720-h264-st-aac-3"
                          withFiletype:@"mov"], @"URL",
                         nil],
                        nil] retain];
}
```

Here we're instantiating an NSArray with items that are of type NSDictionary; each dictionary holds two keys: a title and a URL for the movie. For our movies we're going to use three movie clips we cut from the movie *Elephants Dream*; you'll find these already in your project, or you can add your own movie clips and titles to the viewDidLoad method.[3]

Now that we have our model taken care of and have a controller in place (we'll be making more additions to it in a bit), let's get a view into our application; we're going to do that by adding a table view to the MoviePlayerViewController.m implementation. Add the following code to the bottom of its viewDidLoad method, just before the line of code where player.view is added as a subview:

movieplayer/MoviePlayer3withPlaylist/Classes/MoviePlayerViewController.m

```
PlaylistController *playlist = [[PlaylistController alloc] initWithPlayer:self];
CGRect rect2 = CGRectMake(64, 600, 640, 350);
playlist.view.frame = rect2;
[self.view addSubview:playlist.view];
```

Here we're instantiating a PlaylistController (remember it's a subclass of UITableViewController), setting its frame, and then adding it to the MoviePlayerViewController's view as a subview.

Now let's make a few tweaks to the table view to make it look appropriate for our application. You'll want to add these to the viewDidLoad method back in the PlaylistController:

movieplayer/MoviePlayer3withPlaylist/Classes/PlaylistController.m

```
UITableView *table = self.tableView;
[table setOpaque:NO];
[table setRowHeight:30];
[table setBackgroundColor:[UIColor clearColor]];
[table setSeparatorStyle:UITableViewCellSeparatorStyleNone];
[table setIndicatorStyle:UIScrollViewIndicatorStyleWhite];
```

---

3. Note that this movie is copyright Blender Foundation and can be found at http://www. elephantsdream.org.

These are all aesthetic changes that will result in a nice black table with white letters, no separators, and a gradient background. We also need to alter the way the cells are displayed a bit as well, so we've supplied you with an implementation of tableView:cellForRowAtIndexPath:indexPath: that you can use and take a look at (but isn't really the point of this chapter).

Now we just need some table data so you can see what it looks like. We're going to do that by implementing the UITableViewController data source methods. Let's start with the numberOfSectionsInTableView: and tableView:numberOfRowsInSection: methods, which are straightforward; you're going to return one for the number of sections in the table and return the number of items in your items array for the number of rows:

```
movieplayer/MoviePlayer3withPlaylist/Classes/PlaylistController.m
```

```
- (NSInteger)numberOfSectionsInTableView:
        (UITableView *)tableView {
    return 1;
}

- (NSInteger)tableView:(UITableView *)tableView
        numberOfRowsInSection:(NSInteger)section {
    return [items count];
}
```

Now you're ready for the interesting part: when an item in the playlist is selected, we need to change the movie the player is playing and begin playing it:

```
movieplayer/MoviePlayer3withPlaylist/Classes/PlaylistController.m
```

```
- (void)tableView:(UITableView *)tableView
        didSelectRowAtIndexPath:(NSIndexPath *)indexPath {
    NSURL *url = [[items objectAtIndex:indexPath.row]
                            objectForKey:@"URL"];
    playerController.player.contentURL = url;

    [playerController.player play];
}
```

To do that, here we're using the indexPath of the selected item and determining its row. Once you know the item's row, you can access the content URL of the movie from the items array, which we assign to the url variable. Now, with the URL in hand, we're going to use the contentURL property of the player (that we used in the beginning of the chapter) to point the player to a different movie. And, finally, we call the play method on the player to begin playing the new movie. At this point, compile, run, and give it a try!

In your test run, you probably noticed that if you click an item in the playlist, you get the expected behavior, and the clip plays. But when the clip reaches the end of its playback, the next item in the playlist doesn't begin playing automatically. We're going to fix that now using a notification. Using the NSNotificationCenter, we're going to add the playlist controller as an observer of the MPMoviePlayerPlaybackDidFinishNotification notification. This occurs whenever a movie finishes playing. To do that, add this code to the bottom of your viewDidLoad method:

movieplayer/MoviePlayer3withPlaylist/Classes/PlaylistController.m

```
[[NSNotificationCenter defaultCenter]
 addObserver:self
 selector:@selector(playerPlaybackDidFinish:)
 name:MPMoviePlayerPlaybackDidFinishNotification
 object:nil];
```

Notice this notification, which it triggers, will call the playerPlayback-DidFinish: selector—let's write that now:

movieplayer/MoviePlayer3withPlaylist/Classes/PlaylistController.m

```
- (void) playerPlaybackDidFinish:(NSNotification*)notification {
        UITableViewController *tv = self;
        int rows = [tv.tableView numberOfRowsInSection:0];
        int selectedRow = [self.tableView indexPathForSelectedRow].row;

        if ((selectedRow + 1) < rows) {
                NSIndexPath *path =
                [NSIndexPath indexPathForRow:selectedRow+1
                                                    inSection:0];
                [self.tableView selectRowAtIndexPath:path
                        animated:YES
                        scrollPosition:YES];

                playerController.player.contentURL =
                        [[items objectAtIndex:selectedRow+1]
                          objectForKey:@"URL"];
                [playerController.player play];
        }
}
```

Let's step through this in detail: the first section of code determines the current selected row in the table, which is stored in the select-edRow variable. Next, we step to see whether there is another row in the table beyond the current one, and if so, we create a path to the next row and then ask the table view to show that row as selected using the selectRowAtIndexPath:animated:scrollPosition: method. Note this method does not cause our tableView:didSelectRowAtIndexPath: method to be called, so we still need to assign the content URL and ask the player to play the clip.

That's it. Build and run this code. If this were a commercial implementation, there would be lots of other details we'd want to implement, as well as add functionality such as ad serving, pre-rolls, post-rolls, and so on. But you have the basics of how to approach implementing your own playlist. Now let's move on and see what else we can do with notifications and the player.

7.5 Creating Thumbnails

One of the more interesting capabilities of the MPMoviePlayerController is that it can generate thumbnails of your video's content. The controller provides two methods for generating thumbnails, one synchronous and the other asynchronous. The synchronous call, thumbnailImageAtTime: timeOption:, generates one thumbnail at a time, while the asynchronous version, requestThumbnailImagesAtTimes:timeOption:, can generate multiple thumbnails. If you want to generate a set of thumbnails, you should definitely be using the asynchronous call, given the performance implications of many blocking synchronous calls. Note that Apple currently limits thumbnail generation to video content in the local file system and does not support generation for progressive or streamed content.

Let us briefly examine the synchronous method before moving on to the asynchronous call; you'll find the parameters of the two calls are similar:

```
- (UIImage *)thumbnailImageAtTime:(NSTimeInterval)playbackTime
        timeOption:(MPMovieTimeOption)option
```

The thumbnailImageAtTime method takes a playbackTime and a timeOption as parameters and returns a thumbnail in the form of a UIImage. The playback time is specified as an NSTimeInterval; if you haven't encountered this type before, it is defined as a double where the integral part represents the number of seconds and the fractional part represents fractional seconds.

The timeOption can be one of two values: MPMovieTimeOptionNearestKeyFrame or MPMovieTimeOptionExact. With the MPMovieTimeOptionExact option, the exact time position in the video is used to generate the thumbnail. With the MPMovieTimeOptionNearestKeyFrame option, the nearest keyframe is used instead, which may be several seconds off the time specified. Note that MPMovieTimeOptionNearestKeyFrame is the more efficient option.

Let's now take a look at the asynchronous version:

```
- (void)requestThumbnailImagesAtTimes:(NSArray *)playbackTimes
        timeOption:(MPMovieTimeOption)option
```

There are two main differences here. First, the asynchronous version takes an array of playback times rather than a single time, and second, the method has a return type of void. So, with a return type of void, how do we get our thumbnails from this method? We use notifications. When this method is invoked, it starts processing the thumbnails in the background, and as each image is ready, it posts an MPMoviePlayerThumbnail-ImageRequestDidFinishNotification notification. All we have to do is listen for the notifications and grab the images.

Setting Up a View for Our Thumbnails

You've probably guessed by now that we're going to write code to generate and display thumbnails for our movie application. We're also going to enable those thumbnails so that by touching them, we seek to the corresponding location in the video playback. We first need a good method of managing those thumbnails in our interface. We're going to first tackle the interface and then write the code to generate thumbnails for our entire video file. Before we do that, we should mention that we're going to leave the informational display you just created behind, but you'll see it return in a more sophisticated way in the next chapter.

We'd like a highly interactive way of displaying and interacting with our thumbnails, and for that we're going to use a UIScrollView. As you can see in the following image, we're going to place the thumbnails horizontally next to each other and allow the user to swipe back and forth across them. In addition, we want to support a simple touch on any one thumbnail to bring up the corresponding position in the video in our player. Although that might sound complicated, it takes very little code, including just a small bit of gesture code we've practically copy and pasted from Chapter 3, *Using Gestures*, on page 45.

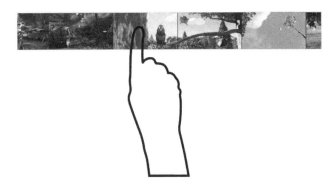

Let's first get the UIScrollView in our interface. Open your MoviePlayerView-Controller.xib nib file, and drag a scroll view into a position just below the player. You'll see our exact size and attributes settings in Figure 7.4, on the following page.

Save your changes in Interface Builder, open the MoviePlayerViewController.h file, add an IBOutlet for the scroll view (as in the following code), and then return to Interface Builder and connect the outlet to your new scroll view:

movieplayer/MoviePlayer4/Classes/MoviePlayerViewController.h

```
@interface MoviePlayerViewController : UIViewController {
        UIView *viewForMovie;
        MPMoviePlayerController *player;
        UIScrollView *thumbnailScrollView;
}

@property (nonatomic, retain) IBOutlet UIView *viewForMovie;
@property (nonatomic, retain) MPMoviePlayerController *player;
@property (nonatomic, retain) IBOutlet UIScrollView *thumbnailScrollView;
- (NSURL *)movieURL;
@end
```

With that out of the way, let's jump into the real code.

Writing the Thumbnail Code

Let's say that we want to generate twenty thumbnails at regular intervals throughout our video (or any other we might view with our application). We need to know the duration of the video, and as we've already seen, we can only be sure we can get an accurate duration after having received the MPMovieDurationAvailableNotification notification. Luckily, we wrote a method named movieDurationAvailable: in the previous section that gets called when the duration is available.

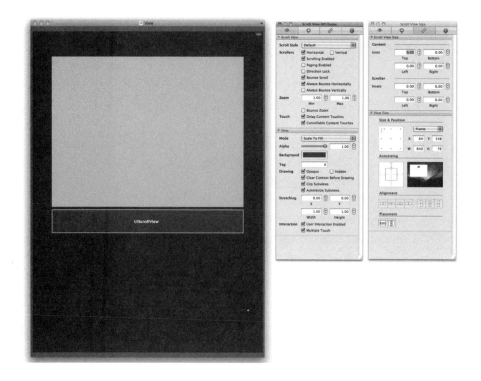

Figure 7.4: Adding a scroll view to display thumbnails

Let's delete the code within movieDurationAvailable: and add the following code:

movieplayer/MoviePlayer4/Classes/MoviePlayerViewController.m

```
- (void) movieDurationAvailable:(NSNotification*)notification {
      float duration = [self.player duration];

      [[NSNotificationCenter defaultCenter]
        addObserver:self
        selector:@selector(playerThumbnailImageRequestDidFinish:)
        name:MPMoviePlayerThumbnailImageRequestDidFinishNotification
        object:nil];

      NSMutableArray *times = [[NSMutableArray alloc] init];
      for(int i = 0; i < 20; i++) {
            float playbackTime = i * duration/20;
            [times addObject:[NSNumber numberWithInt:playbackTime]];
      }
      [self.player
            requestThumbnailImagesAtTimes:times
            timeOption: MPMovieTimeOptionExact];
}
```

Here, we're first grabbing the duration of the video directly from the movie player.[4] Then, before we set up any requests for thumbnails, we make sure to register our interest in MPMoviePlayerThumbnailImageRequestDidFinishNotification notifications, directing any such notifications to the playerThumbnailImageRequestDidFinish: method, which we'll write in a second.

It's time to set up the thumbnail requests. Recall that the requestThumbnailImagesAtTimes:timeOption: method takes an array of times that we'd like to receive thumbnails for. Because our goal is to create twenty thumbnails, we create an NSMutable array and iterate over it twenty times, each time computing an offset based on the duration split into twenty parts. We then call requestThumbnailImagesAtTimes:timeOption: with the array and use the MPMovieTimeOptionExact time option to indicate that we want thumbnails as close to the timecodes as we can get (trading accuracy for efficiency). So, to summarize, we've waited for the player's metadata to be available, and based on that, we've registered to receive thumbnail notifications, as well as gotten a specific asynchronous request in to create twenty thumbnails from the player's video. Now we need to write the playerThumbnailImageRequestDidFinish: method to process the thumbnails as they are generated.

Processing the Thumbnails

Thumbnail generation results in a notification with two items of interest placed into the userInfo dictionary: the value for the MPMoviePlayerThumbnailTimeKey key is an NSNumber object with the timecode of the thumbnail, and the value of the MPMoviePlayerThumbnailImageKey key is the thumbnail image itself. In the code, we retrieve both objects and then use a helper method, makeThumbnailImageViewFromImage:andTimeCode:, to create an image view that we then add as a subview to the scroll view.

movieplayer/MoviePlayer4/Classes/MoviePlayerViewController.m

```
- (void) playerThumbnailImageRequestDidFinish:(NSNotification*)notification {
        NSDictionary *userInfo = [notification userInfo];
        NSNumber *timecode =
                [userInfo objectForKey: MPMoviePlayerThumbnailTimeKey];
        UIImage *image =
                [userInfo objectForKey: MPMoviePlayerThumbnailImageKey];
```

---

4. Recall that we could have retrieved the player object from the notification as well, as we did in the code on page 132.

```
        ImageViewWithTime *imageView =
            [self makeThumbnailImageViewFromImage:image andTimeCode:timecode];

    [thumbnailScrollView addSubview:imageView];
}
```

You'll notice that the makeThumbnailImageViewFromImage:andTimeCode: method returns an ImageViewWithTime object rather than the standard UIImageView. These classes differ only in that the ImageViewWithTime has one additional property named timecode that is used to associate the timecode directly with the thumbnail image view; as you'll see, we'll use this when the user touches the thumbnail. The makeThumbnail-ImageViewFromImage:andTimeCode: method also handles setting up the ImageViewWithTime object's frame so that it is placed within the appropriate position in the scrolling view. If you're interested in the details, we've supplied this method for you in the MoviePlayerViewController.m implementation.

At this point, take a second to compile and generate some thumbnails. Go ahead and run the application, which should generate twenty thumbnails and add them to the scroll view. You should be able to swipe your finger across this view and see them all. One thing that doesn't work is selecting video by touching a thumbnail. Given everything we've done to set this up, we're in good shape to write this code now. In fact, we're going to practically copy and paste some gesture code from Chapter 3, *Using Gestures*, on page 45 to handle the touch event. Here's how:

movieplayer/MoviePlayer4/Classes/MoviePlayerViewController.m

```
- (void) playerThumbnailImageRequestDidFinish:(NSNotification*)notification {
        NSDictionary *userInfo = [notification userInfo];
        NSNumber *timecode =
            [userInfo objectForKey: MPMoviePlayerThumbnailTimeKey];
        UIImage *image =
            [userInfo objectForKey: MPMoviePlayerThumbnailImageKey];

        ImageViewWithTime *imageView =
            [self makeThumbnailImageViewFromImage:image andTimeCode:timecode];

        [thumbnailScrollView addSubview:imageView];

►       UITapGestureRecognizer *tapRecognizer =
►           [[UITapGestureRecognizer alloc]
►               initWithTarget:self action:@selector(handleTapFrom:)];
►       [tapRecognizer setNumberOfTapsRequired:1];
►
```

```
  ▶          [imageView addGestureRecognizer:tapRecognizer];
  ▶          [tapRecognizer release];
  }
```

Here we're creating a single tap gesture recognizer and giving it a target of self with an action of handleTapFrom:. We're then attaching the recognizer to the thumbnail so that each thumbnail, upon a single tap, calls the handleTapFrom: method.

Now we just need to implement the action of the gesture:

movieplayer/MoviePlayer4/Classes/MoviePlayerViewController.m

```
- (void)handleTapFrom:(UITapGestureRecognizer *)recognizer {
        ImageViewWithTime *imageView = recognizer.view;
        self.player.currentPlaybackTime = [imageView.time floatValue];
}
```

The handleTapFrom: method first obtains the view the gesture was recognized on (one of our image views in the scroll view) and then sets the currentPlaybackTime of the player to the timecode stored in the ImageView-WithTime. This has the effect of resetting the play to the video content located at the timecode.

At this point, you're ready to build and run the code again. This time, touching a thumbnail takes you right to the corresponding video content (you can see our test in Figure 7.5, on the next page).

7.6 Looking Ahead

In this chapter, you learned the basics: instantiating the MPMoviePlayer-Controller and providing a view for the video to be rendered, examining properties of video playback, creating observers for notifications about player state, generating thumbnails of video content, and even creating a simple playlist.

In the next chapter, we're going to take things further and look at how you can add views that overlay the video, create custom playback controls, and even look at full-screen video. Finally, in the chapter beyond, we'll look at streaming video content.

Figure 7.5: THE THUMBNAIL VIEW WITH THE MOVIE PLAYER

Chapter 8

Advanced Movie Player

After spending an entire chapter with the MPMoviePlayerController, you now have a lot of knowledge about how to control the player, obtain status information from it, and receive notifications when its state changes. You also know how to generate thumbnails of video content for movies that are stored local on the device.

In this chapter, we're going to take things further by adding interactivity to the player, first by implementing time-based messages that overlay the video and then by creating a set of custom playback controls. We'll then add some finishing touches by exploring the handling of full-screen video.

8.1 Video Shoutouts

The MPMoviePlayerController's view can be used for more than just displaying video content. Although you should treat this view carefully and not alter any of its properties directly, you can add your own subviews, which gives us a way to overlay content over the video.

In this section, we're going to use this capability to create a simple shoutout system that allows us to display visual callouts at specific times throughout the video playback—if you've see the VH-1 style of "pop-up" video, you know where we're going (check out Figure 8.1, on the following page for a preview). Toward that goal, we've placed a CommentView class into the MoviePlayer5 project that displays a thought bubble-style graphic, complete with an alpha shadow and a text overlay (feel free to check it out if you're interested in the code, but it's a little off-topic for our discussion here).

Figure 8.1: THE THUMBNAIL VIEW WITH THE MOVIE PLAYER

Before we start coding, keep in mind that our aim is to demonstrate adding subviews to videos, not to implement a sophisticated system of maintaining shoutout text and times. In fact, our model and logic around the shoutouts might be called embarrassingly simple. As simple as it is, let's take a look at the model:

movieplayer/MoviePlayer5/Classes/MoviePlayerViewController.m

```
- (void)viewDidLoad {
    [super viewDidLoad];

    shoutOutTexts = [[NSArray
        arrayWithObjects:
            @"This film\nwas rendered using\ncloud computing ",
            @"Look out\nFrank, Rinky\nand Gamera!",
            nil] retain];
```

```
        shoutOutTimes = [[NSArray
              arrayWithObjects:
                         [[NSNumber alloc] initWithInt: 2],
                         [[NSNumber alloc] initWithInt: 325],
                         nil] retain];

        position = 0;

        // rest of viewDidLoad goes here
}
```

To store the shoutouts, we're using two simple arrays: one for holding the timecode at which the shoutout should appear and one for holding the text of the shoutout. For instance, we might store "Hello Ma!" and 17 to indicate that the text "Hello Ma!" should be displayed 17 seconds into the video playback. Note that we're also assuming the times are in sequential order, with the later times after the earlier times. We've also added an integer instance variable, position, that we're setting to zero here (we'll get back to this in a bit) to keep track of the current shoutout.

Now, to know when to display shoutouts, we need to keep an eye on the video playback. To do that, let's use the NSTimer class to set up a call to a method on a regular interval; add this code in the viewDidLoad method, just below the shoutout array instantiations:

movieplayer/MoviePlayer5/Classes/MoviePlayerViewController.m

```
[NSTimer
 scheduledTimerWithTimeInterval:1.0f
 target:self
 selector:@selector(checkShoutouts:)
 userInfo:nil
 repeats:YES];
```

Here we're using the NSTimer to schedule a method call in one second, targeting the checkShoutouts method in this class. Further, we'd like this timer to keep repeating the method call every second.

Now we need to write the checkShoutouts method that is called by the timer. Here's how it is going to work: we're going to maintain an instance variable called position that acts as a pointer to the next shoutout to be displayed. Every time the checkShoutouts method is called by the timer, we're going to compare the player's currentPlaybackTime against the current shoutout time, and if the currentPlaybackTime is equal to or less than the current shoutout time, we're going to display the shoutout and increment the position. We've taken the time comparison logic and abstracted it into a method called isTimeForNextShoutout:

movieplayer/MoviePlayer5/Classes/MoviePlayerViewController.m

```
-(BOOL)isTimeForNextShoutout {
        int count = [shoutOutTimes count];
        if (position < count) {
                int timecode = [[shoutOutTimes
                             objectAtIndex:position] intValue];
                if (self.player.currentPlaybackTime >= timecode) {
                        return YES;
                }
        }
        return NO;
}
```

Let's use this method to write the checkShoutouts:. First, we need to see whether there is a new shoutout to display, and if so, we instantiate a CommentView with the text of the shoutout and add it as a subview to the player's view. Think about what's happening here: we've just taken a view and added it not to our application's primary view but rather to the video display view of the player—otherwise known as the MPMoviePlayerController. This has the effect of displaying the view directly on top of the video content, which we'll see running in a minute.

movieplayer/MoviePlayer5/Classes/MoviePlayerViewController.m

```
- (void)checkShoutouts:(NSTimer*)theTimer {
        if ([self isTimeForNextShoutout]) {
                CommentView *commentView = [[CommentView alloc]
                        initWithText:[shoutOutTexts objectAtIndex:position++]];

                [self.player.view addSubview:commentView];

                [NSTimer scheduledTimerWithTimeInterval:4.0f
                        target:self
                        selector:@selector(removeView:)
                        userInfo:commentView
                        repeats:NO];
        }
}
```

Only one task is left—at some point, we need to remove the shoutout. We're going to create another NSTimer, one that will fire after four seconds. We're also going to fill the userInfo parameter, which is going to get passed to the action method with our shoutout view.

For the action, we're going to call removeView after four seconds. What happens in removeView is very simple: we get a reference to the shoutout view in the userInfo parameter and remove it from its superview (in other words, from the MPMoviePlayerController's video view).

```
movieplayer/MoviePlayer5/Classes/MoviePlayerViewController.m
- (void)removeView:(NSTimer*)theTimer {
        UIView *view = [theTimer userInfo];
        [view removeFromSuperview];
}
```

That wraps up our shoutout code. Compile, run the code, and enjoy. Notice the nice alpha-blended shadows right over top of the video. You can make up your own shoutouts or, even better, implement your own user-generated shoutout system.

8.2 Implementing Custom Playback Controls

At this point, we have a few things under our belt: getting status information from the player, receiving notifications, and adding subviews to the video display. You're now going to take that knowledge and use it to build your own custom controls for the player. Why would you want to do that? Well, let's take a look at Apple's built-in controls:

Apple provides a solid implementation of the playback controls, including a play/pause button, a slider for scrubbing through the video, a time display, and a full-screen button. Not bad, but aren't there times when you might want to give your users additional functionality (say social networking options) or improve the look of the controls or brand them to fit a particular theme in your content?

We think so, and toward that goal, we're going to explore this space by creating some playback controls in the form of a heads-up display that directly overlays the video content.

Volume Control

You might have noticed that we've omitted a volume control in our design (as has Apple in its design), which may seem odd given users often expect a volume slider within playback controls. That said, Apple provides no direct method of controlling the MPMoviePlayerController's volume and expects the user to adjust the volume through the physical volume button on the device.

Here's what we have in mind:

For a first cut, that's an improvement, isn't it? Now, we haven't gone crazy with branding or radically changed the controls—we'll leave that to you and your applications—but we have implemented a more immersive control that is semitransparent and sits right in the middle of the video. We provide all the basics Apple does, and we've even hinted at some new functionality that could be added (like the thought bubbles representing a sharing capability, which we won't implement, but it is there waiting for you). Note that we've also supplied our own custom version of the slider, rather than the default Apple look and feel.

Creating comps (graphic representations) of a new playback control is fairly easy, but implementing a playback control that functions as well as Apple's takes a bit of careful work. Let's think about what a playback control needs to do to function properly. We need to know the state of the player. Is it playing? Paused? Is the user seeking within the video? Where is the playback location? Have we adjusted the time and slider playback position? Is the user trying to change the state of the player (say, from play to paused)? Does the user want to go to full-screen? What do we do if the playback reaches the end of the video? There are obviously a lot of details, and it's pretty clear our implementation could get quite complex, but given a lot of the tools we've already learned, we can keep our design fairly small and simple. Over the next few pages, we're going to dive into each one of these details and come up for air once everything is working.

Creating the View

We're going to start by building the playback control as its own view and view controller and then integrate it into the movie player's video view. Begin by opening the movieplayer/MoviePlayer6 project, and you'll notice we've supplied a few new items since our last project: some new images in the Images group and also a new nib file named PlaybackView-Controller.xib. Double-click the nib file to open it in Interface Builder, and you'll see the following interface:

If you refer to the comp of the playback controls we just looked at, you'll see that things look a little different: first, the slider looks like Apple's conventional slider, not our custom one—that's OK; in a bit, we'll get the look we want programmatically. The interface also looks solid gray, and we were going for a nice, transparent control. This is OK too, because the nib interface is sitting against the solid white background, making it hard to tell that it's actually transparent. Once we get this interface placed over top of the video, you'll see the background is semitransparent (for more information on semitransparent views, see the sidebar on page 153).

Take a few minutes to explore this nib; there's a lot here. Check out the views we've added and the associated text and images we've used. Note, for instance, that the play/pause button has two states and an image representing each. You'll find it helpful in Interface Builder to use the list view to take a look at what we've done. You should see this:

Doing a quick survey, you should see the background image that acts as the visual container for all the controls. Then we have several UILabelViews; some act as simple text labels in the interface, and others will be used to display real-time information such as the time and status. You'll also see an UISlider; this is our control for scrubbing (also known as a scroll or progress bar) through video.

Next, you'll find a few buttons: the play/pause button we've already mentioned that toggles between the play and pause states, the full-screen button will take the display into full-screen playback of video, and a share button (in the form of two thought bubbles) that we'll leave as something you could add to your own playback control (our point isn't to implement that functionality but to show that you can extend the basic controls to add new functionality).

So, we've done all the design work in Interface Builder for you; now comes the real work of breathing life into it—and to do that, let's create some IBActions and IBOutlets and then wire a controller to this view.

Creating the Controller

Back in Xcode, create a view controller for the nib—choose File > New File..., and create a UIViewController subclass. You'll want to make sure

Creating the Semitransparent Interface

In general, you can make any interface element semitransparent by setting its alpha value less than 1.0. A setting of 0 is fully transparent, or invisible. Here's how we create the semitransparent background shell for our interface:

1. Uncheck the opaque setting on the PlaybackViewController's view.

2. Select the view's background color, and set its alpha to 0. These two steps ensure that we can see through the entire view we're creating; otherwise, the PlaybackViewController's view would appear as a solid white view.

3. Create your interface background in a tool such as Photoshop, set its alpha value to semitransparent (in our case, about .65), and then save the image in PNG format.

4. Add the image to your main project, and create an UIImageView object in Interface Builder to hold the image.

Note that you could also create a similar background programmatically, but you might choose an image if your interface includes a fair amount of realism or design that isn't easily approached algorithmically.

"With XIB for user interface" and "UITableViewController subclass" are unchecked. Call the controller PlaybackViewController.m, and click Finish. Then open PlaybackViewController.h, and add the following IBOutlets (one for each view we'll need access to in our controller code):

movieplayer/MoviePlayer6Start/Classes/PlaybackViewController.h

```
@interface PlaybackViewController : UIViewController {
        IBOutlet UISlider *playbackSlider;
        IBOutlet UIButton *playPauseButton;
        IBOutlet UIButton *fullscreenButton;
        IBOutlet UILabel *statusLabel;
        IBOutlet UILabel *timeLabel;
}
```

Return to Interface Builder, and connect each outlet to its appropriate view in the nib file. You'll also want to click File's Owner and set its class on the Identity tab to PlaybackViewController.

For a little instant gratification, let's get this view hooked up to our video player, give the code a spin by running it, and then we'll come back and start implementing its behavior. Open the MoviePlayerViewController.m, and add the following code to the bottom of the viewDidLoad method:

movieplayer/MoviePlayer6Start/Classes/MoviePlayerViewController.m

```
self.player.controlStyle = MPMovieControlStyleNone;
PlaybackViewController *controls =
        [[PlaybackViewController alloc] init];
CGRect rect = controls.view.frame;
rect.origin.y = 170;
rect.origin.x = 90;
controls.view.frame = rect;
[self.player.view  addSubview:controls.view];
```

Let's step through this. First, we set the controlStyle property of the movie player, which controls the style of its built-in controls. We set this property to MPMovieControlStyleNone, which effectively removes all the built-in controls. If we didn't do this, we'd be presenting the user with two sets of controls (ours and Apple's). Next, we instantiate a PlaybackViewController, adjusting its frame to fit nicely inside the movie view, and then add it to the player's view as a subview.

Compile and run this code. You should see a functioning (but not yet functional) set of controls appear over the video content. For now we're going to leave the playback control displayed over the video content at all times; we'll come back later and make the controls appear only when the user touches within the video bounds (and similarly, make it disappear when they've stopped interacting with it). Now that you have your playback control positioned and visible, let's implement it.

8.3 Implementing the Controls

Let's start with the task of getting the play/pause button working. To do this, we first need to give our playback controls a reference to the player—so, add a new property to the PlaybackViewController.h header file:

movieplayer/MoviePlayer6Start/Classes/PlaybackViewController.h

```
MPMoviePlayerController *player;
```

Then add a new initialization method, called initWithPlayer:, to the PlaybackViewController.m implementation file.

```
movieplayer/MoviePlayer6Start/Classes/PlaybackViewController.m
```

```
-(id)initWithPlayer:(MPMoviePlayerController *)thePlayer {
        self = [super init];
        if (nil != self) {
                player = thePlayer;
        }
        return self;
}
```

Here all we're doing beyond calling the init method in the superclass is assigning the player to a property in the PlaybackViewController, which we'll soon use. Now you'll need to update the viewDidLoad: method in MoviePlayerController.m by replacing its call to init with initWithPlayer: and passing it self.player:

```
movieplayer/MoviePlayer6Start/Classes/MoviePlayerViewController.m
```

```
PlaybackViewController *controls =
        [[PlaybackViewController alloc] initWithPlayer:self.player];
```

Now we're ready to write the actual code for the play/pause button. Given this is a UIButton, we're going to need an action to call when the button is touched; add an action called handlePlayPause: to the Playback-ViewController.m implementation file:

```
movieplayer/MoviePlayer6Start/Classes/PlaybackViewController.m
```

```
-(IBAction)handlePlayAndPauseButton:(id)sender {
        UIButton *button = (UIButton *)sender;
        if (button.selected) {
                button.selected = NO;
                [player play];
        } else {
                button.selected = YES;
                [player pause];
        }
}
```

Remember when we explored the interface in Interface Builder that the button has two states, a play state (the unselected state) and a pause state (the selected state). If the button is in the selected state, it's paused, so we change the state to unselected and ask the player to play the video. Likewise, if the button is in the unselected state, we set the state to selected and then ask the player to pause the video.

Now you need to wire the button to this action, so, in Interface Builder, connect the play UIButton to the handlePlayPause: method by dragging to File's Owner. That's it; build and run the code, and try the play/pause button.

8.4 Managing Playback Time

We have a few aspects of the interface that deal with time: the time
label, which we intend to use to display both the current time and the
total duration of the video, and also the slider, which will be updated as
the video progresses (and allows the user to scrub through the video).
Let's start by writing the code to update the time label, which is going
to be very similar to code you wrote in the previous chapter.

If you'll recall, we can set up an MPMovieDurationAvailableNotification notification and then start tracking the time of the video once we're sure the
player knows the duration of the video (we'll use this in a bit to update
the slider as well). To do this, open PlaybackViewController.m, and add
this code in the initWithPlayer method:

movieplayer/MoviePlayer6Start/Classes/PlaybackViewController.m

```
-(id)initWithPlayer:(MPMoviePlayerController *)thePlayer {
        self = [super init];
        if (nil != self) {
                player = thePlayer;
▶               [[NSNotificationCenter defaultCenter]
▶                addObserver:self
▶                selector:@selector(movieDurationAvailable:)
▶                name:MPMovieDurationAvailableNotification
▶                object:nil];
        }
        return self;
}
```

Here we've set up the notification to call movieDurationAvailable: when the
player knows the video's duration. Let's write the movieDurationAvailable:
method:

movieplayer/MoviePlayer6Start/Classes/PlaybackViewController.m

```
- (void) movieDurationAvailable:(NSNotification*)notification {
        if (playbackTimer == nil) {
                playbackTimer =
                        [NSTimer scheduledTimerWithTimeInterval:1.0f
                                target:self
                                selector:@selector(updatePlaybackTime:)
                                userInfo:nil
                                repeats:YES];
        }
}
```

This should look familiar. We're going to set up a timer that tracks the
time of the video playback by calling the updatePlaybackTime: method

every second. Enter this method into the controller file, and then let's take a look at the updatePlaybackTime: method:

movieplayer/MoviePlayer6Start/Classes/PlaybackViewController.m

```
- (void)updatePlaybackTime:(NSTimer*)theTimer {
                float playbackTime = player.currentPlaybackTime;
                float duration = player.duration;

                timeLabel.text = [NSString stringWithFormat:
                                            @"%.f of %.f secs",
                                            playbackTime,
                                            duration];
}
```

This should look familiar as well: we're grabbing the duration and current playback time from the player, formatting it, and setting the text of the timeLabel outlet.

While we're at it, let's add a bit of status information to the interface as well, using the MPMoviePlayerPlaybackStateDidChangeNotification notification we're also familiar with. Set up the notification in the initWithPlayer: method like this:

movieplayer/MoviePlayer6Start/Classes/PlaybackViewController.m

```
[[NSNotificationCenter defaultCenter]
 addObserver:self
 selector:@selector(playerPlaybackStateDidChange:)
 name:MPMoviePlayerPlaybackStateDidChangeNotification
 object:nil];
```

Now let's define the playerPlaybackStateDidChange: method:

movieplayer/MoviePlayer6Start/Classes/PlaybackViewController.m

```
- (void) playerPlaybackStateDidChange:(NSNotification*)notification {
      if ([player playbackState]
                    == MPMoviePlaybackStatePaused) {
            statusLabel.text = @"Paused...";
            playPauseButton.selected = YES;

      } else if ([player playbackState]
                    == MPMoviePlaybackStatePlaying) {
            statusLabel.text = @"Playing";
            playPauseButton.selected = NO;
      } else if ([player playbackState]
                    == MPMoviePlaybackStateStopped) {
            statusLabel.text = @"Stopped";
            playPauseButton.selected = NO;
      }
}
```

The main purpose of this code is to update our status label with the current state of the player (playing, paused, stopped). To accomplish this, we simply check the status of the player and update the label with the appropriate text. Note that in the case of the paused and play states, we're also setting the state of the pause/play button. Why? Remember, a state change could occur because some other part of our application that has access to the video player makes a change to its state. If this happens, our buttons have no idea that the state has changed. So, we listen for this notification and update them ourselves. As you'll see in the upcoming section, the scrubber pauses the video as the user scrubs, and without this notification code, the play/pause button would incorrectly show the video as playing while we're scrubbing.

8.5 Implementing a Video Scrubber

We're getting there. All that's left to implement is the slider and the full-screen button. The slider, as you might expect, is the most complicated piece to implement, because we have to track its progress and update things appropriately. Actually, our first task is changing its appearance to give it the custom look we want. Let's start there.

Add the following code to the viewDidLoad: method in the playback controller:

movieplayer/MoviePlayer6Start/Classes/PlaybackViewController.m

```
    [playbackSlider
     setThumbImage:[UIImage imageNamed:@"thumb.png"]
     forState:UIControlStateNormal];
    UIImage *stretchLeftTrack =
            [[UIImage imageNamed:@"leftslider.png"]
             stretchableImageWithLeftCapWidth:5.0
             topCapHeight:0.0];
    UIImage *stretchRightTrack =
            [[UIImage imageNamed:@"rightslider.png"]
             stretchableImageWithLeftCapWidth:5.0
             topCapHeight:0.0];
    [playbackSlider setMinimumTrackImage:stretchLeftTrack
            forState:UIControlStateNormal];
    [playbackSlider setMaximumTrackImage:stretchRightTrack
            forState:UIControlStateNormal];
}
```

Although this code looks a bit complex, it's simply supplying a few images to the slider to give it a different look. More specifically, we're supplying three images: one for the thumb of the slider and two others that represent the left and right troughs of the slider. At this point, you can compile, build, and see your new slider in action (it will function but obviously have no effect on the controls or video).

Now we need to take care of a bit of housekeeping. To have a functioning slider, we need to know the minimum and maximum values of the slider. We know the minimum value is going to be zero seconds, but for the maximum, we need the total duration of the video. What better place to set that up than the movieDurationAvailable: method that we just wrote?

movieplayer/MoviePlayer6Start/Classes/PlaybackViewController.m

```
- (void) movieDurationAvailable:(NSNotification*)notification {
        if (playbackTimer == nil) {
                playbackTimer =
                        [NSTimer scheduledTimerWithTimeInterval:1.0f
                                target:self
                                selector:@selector(updatePlaybackTime:)
                                userInfo:nil
                                repeats:YES];
        }
        playbackSlider.minimumValue = 0.0;
        playbackSlider.maximumValue = [player duration];
}
```

That should work well—as soon as we have the video loaded to the point where we know the duration, the slider's minimum and maximum values will be set.

Now that we have the range of values, we need the slider to track the progress of the video as it plays. Because we already have a method that tracks the video's progress over time (the updatePlaybackTime: method), we simply update the slider's value when this method is called:

movieplayer/MoviePlayer6Start/Classes/PlaybackViewController.m

```
- (void)updatePlaybackTime:(NSTimer*)theTimer {
                float playbackTime = player.currentPlaybackTime;
                float duration = player.duration;

                timeLabel.text = [NSString stringWithFormat:
                                                @"%.f of %.f secs",
                                                playbackTime,
                                                duration];
                playbackSlider.value = playbackTime;
}
```

It's a good time to build and run your application again. This time, you should see the slider progressing as the movie plays, but you still won't be able to adjust the position of the video with the slider. It's time to implement that functionality now. To do that, we must return to Interface Builder and wire up two additional actions. Enter the declarations for the actions in the playback control header file, and then open the player control nib. Here are the declarations:

movieplayer/MoviePlayer6Start/Classes/PlaybackViewController.h

```
-(IBAction)playbackSliderMoved:(UISlider *)sender;
-(IBAction)playbackSliderDone:(UISlider *)sender;
```

To wire things up, select the UISlider view in the nib, and bring up the inspector's Connections tab. You'll want to make two connections from this tab back to the File's Owner: connect from the Touch Up Inside event to the playbackSliderDone: method and from the Value Changed event to the playbackSliderMoved: method. Your inspector tab should look like this:

The former event occurs when the user is finished with the slider and lifts his finger. The latter event occurs as the user slides his finger back and forth within the slider. Now we're going to implement the behavior for each of these events, starting with the playbackSliderMoved: method.

moviepiayer/MoviePiayer6Start/Classes/PlaybackViewController.m

```
- (IBAction)playbackSliderMoved:(UISlider *)sender {
        if (player.playbackState != MPMoviePlaybackStatePaused) {
                [player pause];
        }
        player.currentPlaybackTime = sender.value;

        timeLabel.text = [NSString stringWithFormat:
                                        @"%.f of %.f secs",
                                        sender.value, player.duration];
        sliding = YES;
}
```

If the player isn't in a paused state, we pause it. If we leave the player playing in this state, we'll be in a constant tug of war between the progression of the video and the slider. Next, set the current player's currentPlaybackTime to the value of the slider, which repositions the actual playback of the video player. Then we update the time label to the new position. Finally, we introduce a new boolean property called sliding that tracks whether we are currently using the slider (don't forget to add this instance variable to the PlaybackViewController header file). We're going to see the reason we need this boolean tracking the slider in just a bit.

Before we move on, let's review: when you first touch the slider, the video is first paused, and then the playback position of the video changes as we slide the slider through its range of minimum (0) and maximum (the video's duration) values. As we do that, we update the time label of the control and also ensure the boolean instance variable slider is set to YES as soon as we start using the slider. Let's take care of what happens when the user lifts her finger from the slider:

moviepiayer/MoviePiayer6Start/Classes/PlaybackViewController.m

```
- (IBAction)playbackSliderDone:(UISlider *)sender
{
        sliding = NO;

        if (player.playbackState != MPMoviePlaybackStatePlaying) {
                [player play];
        }
}
```

As it turns out, this method is straightforward. All we need to do is set the sliding property to NO and restart the paused video by sending the player the play message when the user lifts her finger.

That's it, give it a try (just a little heads up that the slider is going to work but not exactly as we'd like).

> **Another Problem with the Slider**
>
> If you've played with the slider, you might have noticed another issue: sometimes when you lift your finger, the video stays paused and doesn't restart playing. Can you think of a reason this might happen? Might this be a bug in the UISlider that isn't generating the ending Touch Up Inside event? Not so fast. Take a look at the other UISlider events, and see whether you can spot the potential problem (and identify the solution).

OK, you knew we put that boolean in there for a reason. You might have noticed a slightly strange behavior with the slider: as you scrub through the range of the slider, every second the position bounces back to the previous position of the slider. Why? It's because the updatePlayback-Time: method is being called every second, and every time it is called, it updates the slider's value. In the case, where we're in the act of sliding, we'd rather this not happen. Using the sliding boolean, can you now fix this? Here's how we did:

movieplayer/MoviePlayer6Start/Classes/PlaybackViewController.m

```
- (void)updatePlaybackTime:(NSTimer*)theTimer {
        if (!sliding) {
                float playbackTime = player.currentPlaybackTime;
                float duration = player.duration;

                timeLabel.text = [NSString stringWithFormat:
                                            @"%.f of %.f secs",
                                            playbackTime,
                                            duration];
                playbackSlider.value = playbackTime;
        }
}
```

That concludes the slider implementation. Compile, and give it a good testing. Now it's time to add a little polish.

8.6 Making the Playback Control Dynamic

We have almost all the basics of the playback control working, and it's time to concentrate on the details of how the control reveals itself (rather than being on-screen all the time as we have it now). Here's the behavior we'd like: when the user taps within the bounds of the video view, the playback controls should gradually fade in and stay visible until the controls haven't been touched for four seconds, and then they should fade away, fully revealing the video again.

Our first task is to alter our implementation so the user doesn't see the controls when the application begins. To do that, we're just going to set their opacity to transparent by setting the alpha of the playback controller's view to 0 (which will make all subviews transparent). This is easily done in the viewDidLoad: method within your PlaybackViewController class; you can add this line to the bottom of the method:

```
self.view.alpha = 0.0;
```

Try building and running your application at this point—you'll see that the playback controls have disappeared. Don't worry; we'll get them back.

From here, things get a little more interesting. You're going to have to determine when the controls should be displayed, give them a little sparkle through an animation as they reveal themselves, and then carefully manage them when they are put away. Done right, this will give your playback controls a professional feel. Done wrong, you are going to have very frustrated users.

The first task we need to tackle is sensing the taps of the user within the video bounds. Given that the MPMoviePlayerController's view is to be treated as an opaque view that is off-limits (other than adding subviews), we're going to create our own UIView, called touchView, place it over the video (which we're well versed at now), and then sense taps on that view. To do that, add the following code at the bottom of the PlaybackViewController's viewDidLoad: method:

movieplayer/MoviePlayer6Start/Classes/PlaybackViewController.m

```
UIView *touchView = [[[UIView alloc] init] autorelease];
touchView.frame = player.view.frame;
[player.view addSubview:touchView];
```

Now let's add a simple one-tap gesture to the view:

movieplayer/MoviePlayer6Start/Classes/PlaybackViewController.m

```
UITapGestureRecognizer *tapRecognizer =
[[[UITapGestureRecognizer alloc]
        initWithTarget:self action:@selector(handleTapFrom:)]
 autorelease];
[tapRecognizer setNumberOfTapsRequired:1];
[touchView addGestureRecognizer:tapRecognizer];
```

Here, we've created a tap gesture recognizer using handleTapFrom: as its action and attached it to the touchView. Let's write the handleTapFrom: method now:

movieplayer/MoviePlayer6Start/Classes/PlaybackViewController.m

```
- (void)handleTapFrom:(UITapGestureRecognizer *)recognizer {
        [UIView beginAnimations:nil context:nil];
        [UIView setAnimationDuration:1.5];
        self.view.alpha = 1.0;
        [UIView commitAnimations];
        [self setControlsTimer];
}
```

The handleTapFrom: method performs two functions: first, it sets up an animation to take the PlaybackViewController's view from an alpha value of 0 to a value of 1 over a duration of one and a half seconds. This results in a nice fade-in effect for the playback controls.

The other function of the handleTapFrom: method is to set up a timer that fires after four seconds. To set up the timer, it calls the method setControlsTimer:

movieplayer/MoviePlayer6Start/Classes/PlaybackViewController.m

```
-(void)setControlsTimer {
        if (controlsTimer) {
                [controlsTimer invalidate];
                [controlsTimer release];
                controlsTimer = nil;
        }
        controlsTimer = [[NSTimer timerWithTimeInterval:4.0
                target:self
                selector:@selector(handleControlsTimer:)
                userInfo:nil
                repeats:NO] retain];
        [[NSRunLoop currentRunLoop]
          addTimer:controlsTimer
          forMode:NSDefaultRunLoopMode];
}
```

This method might look a little more complex than you were anticipating; let's walk through it in detail. Here, we first check a new property, controlsTimer, which, if referencing an active timer, is first invalidated and then released. Why is this code here? Think about it this way: if a user taps within the bounds of the video area, we want to set a timer to fire in four seconds, but if the user taps again, there's already a timer active—so we need to invalidate that timer. Moving on in the code, whether or not there is an active timer, we must create another timer that is set four seconds ahead. The remaining code in this method does that, using the handleControlsTimer: method as its selector when the timer fires. Let's write this method, handleControlsTimer:, which actually passes off its responsibility to removeControls:. Both are listed here:

movieplayer/MoviePlayer6Start/Classes/PlaybackViewController.m

```
- (void)handleControlsTimer:(NSTimer *)timer {
        [self removeControls];
        [controlsTimer release];
        controlsTimer = nil;
}
```

movieplayer/MoviePlayer6Start/Classes/PlaybackViewController.m

```
-(void)removeControls {
        [UIView beginAnimations:nil context:nil];
        [UIView setAnimationDuration:1.5];
        self.view.alpha = 0.0;
        [UIView commitAnimations];
}
```

The removeControls: method simply hides the playback controls in the same way they were originally revealed, with the order reversed: by setting the alpha back to zero within an animation block, giving us a new fade-out effect.

We're not quite done yet, but compile this code, and give it a try. You'll notice the control appears in a nice way but also disappears no matter what in four seconds, which isn't quite right. We want the controls to stick around as long as there's activity and the user is touching them in some way.

We can fix this fairly easily. We just need to add this in a few choice places:

```
[self setControlsTimer];
```

We added this code to the end of the playbackSliderMoved: and handle-PlayAndPauseButton: methods. This has the effect of resetting the timer any time the play/pause button or the slider is touched. Add a call to setControlsTimer:, and give the application a try; you should find it is working as expected now.

Extra Credit: A Nagging Detail

It's customary for some video players to leave the playback controls displayed as long as the pause button is engaged. Now that the playback controls are implemented, when you press the pause button, the controls disappear four seconds later (give it a try). How would you change the implementation to keep the controls on the screen until the play button (or another button) is pressed? Think about it, and give it a shot before you look at our solution here:

`movieplayer/MoviePlayer6Full/Classes/PlaybackViewController.m`

```
-(IBAction)handlePlayAndPauseButton:(id)sender {
        UIButton *button = (UIButton *)sender;
        if (button.selected) {
                button.selected = NO;
                [player play];
                [self setControlsTimer];
        } else {
                button.selected = YES;
                [player pause];
                [controlsTimer invalidate];
                [controlsTimer release];
                controlsTimer = nil;
        }
}
```

8.7 Handling Full-Screen

In-application video is great on the iPad, don't you think? But it's even better when viewing full-screen; isn't it time to get that full-screen button working? To do so, add an IBAction to your PlaybackViewController.h header file called handleFullscreenButton, and then, using Interface Builder, connect the full-screen button in the player control to this action. Once you've done that, entering full-screen is as easy as calling the setFullscreen:animated method, like this:

`movieplayer/MoviePlayer6Full/Classes/PlaybackViewController.m`

```
-(IBAction)handleFullscreenButton {
        [player setFullscreen:YES animated:YES];
}
```

If you jumped ahead and compiled and ran this code, you probably noticed a little problem: once you're in full-screen mode, there are no player controls. Why? We added our player controls to be the subview of the in-app view; when the player goes full-screen, it is making use of another view to do this. Moving the custom controls to this view requires getting access to the iPad's mainScreen, something we're going to do in Chapter 10, *Displaying Content on Another Screen*. Rather than go down that path, let's fully explore the API around full-screen mode and use notifications to reenable the default controls when the video is full-screen.

Let's start by registering to receive two notifications within the initWith-Player: method of the PlaybackViewController.m file; just add this code to the bottom of the method:

movieplayer/MoviePlayer6Full/Classes/PlaybackViewController.m

```
[[NSNotificationCenter defaultCenter]
 addObserver:self
 selector:@selector(playerWillExitFullscreen:)
 name:MPMoviePlayerWillExitFullscreenNotification
 object:nil];

[[NSNotificationCenter defaultCenter]
 addObserver:self
 selector:@selector(playerDidEnterFullscreen:)
 name:MPMoviePlayerDidEnterFullscreenNotification
 object:nil];
```

Now let's define the playerDidEnterFullscreen: method; in this method, we need to set the player control style to a style such as MPMovieControl-StyleDefault, which includes controls and a way to exit full-screen:

movieplayer/MoviePlayer6Full/Classes/PlaybackViewController.m

```
- (void) playerDidEnterFullscreen:(NSNotification*)notification {
        player.controlStyle = MPMovieControlStyleDefault;
}
```

However, when we exit full-screen, we don't want to have our custom controls and the default control style because we'll get two sets of conflicting controls. Let's use our other notification handled to set the control style back to none:

movieplayer/MoviePlayer6Full/Classes/PlaybackViewController.m

```
- (void) playerWillExitFullscreen:(NSNotification*)notification {
        player.controlStyle = MPMovieControlStyleNone;
}
```

Compile and run, and you should have a fully functional full-screen viewing experience.

8.8 Summary

If you look back over the past two chapters, we've covered a lot of ground. You're now in a position to create your own sophisticated video-viewing experience or include video in your application in a highly integrated and interactive manner.

There is one piece we're still missing, however: dealing with video that is streamed from the Internet, and that's what we're going to tackle now, in the next chapter.

Chapter 9

Apple's HTTP Live Streaming

As you've seen in the previous two chapters, playing video from the application bundle is straightforward (and there will certainly be applications for which embedding your video content is appropriate); using bundled video has also allowed us to focus on creating great video experiences without worrying about issues such as network connections, servers, latency, and bandwidth issues. However, for many applications, if not most, you'll need to stream video, over the network, to the iPad.

In this chapter, we're going to explore iPad video streaming—why you need it, what it means, how it differs from locally played video, and how to accomplish it. You'll be able to apply almost everything you learned in the previous two chapters, with a few exceptions, but we're also going to add a few more bits of knowledge that you'll need to create video experiences in a networked environment.

9.1 Progressive vs. Streamed Video

Let's first start with a common confusion: progressive vs. streamed video. With progressively delivered video, you place a video asset on a web server and then ask the client to retrieve it via the HTTP protocol. Using this method, the media player is essentially downloading the asset and playing it back (usually in the form of a locally cached file) as it gets content.

Progressive download has its advantages; it's easy, and it works by placing your video file on any web server. It also has disadvantages: it can be costly (often you download a lot more content than the user ever views), and it gives you no way to adjust the bit rate of the content as the user views the video. Also, Apple places restrictions on your applications—if your video exceeds either ten minutes in duration or 5MB of data in a five-minute period, you must use streaming instead of progressive download. The reason? Streaming avoids the pitfalls we just mentioned with progressive download and allows us to adjust the playback bit rate as needed, depending on the user's network conditions. The disadvantage? It has traditionally required proprietary infrastructure and protocols to pull off streaming. Apple's improved on that with its HTTP-based streaming protocol. Let's take a look.

9.2 Apple's HTTP-Based Streaming Protocol

Apple has created an open standards-based protocol called the HTTP Live Streaming protocol (HLS for short). Given that Apple has based the protocol on HTTP, the standard transport protocol used by all browsers and web servers, you're going to be able to place your video content on any garden-variety web server to be streamed to the iPad. Also, don't be confused by "Live" in the name of HLS; although HLS supports the streaming of live content, such as, say, a sports event or concert (with the help of real-time encoders available commercially on the market), it also works for video-on-demand types of applications, where you have prerecorded video content you'd like to stream to your users.

How HTTP Live Streaming Works

Most commercial streaming solutions transport your video content over one or more open sockets using a proprietary protocol. Supporting these proprietary solutions typically requires the setup and maintenance of large server farms that are dedicated to the streaming protocol (often hosted on content delivery networks).

HLS uses a different approach where your video is broken into many small segments and then stored on conventional web servers. Video players in the client use the conventional HTTP protocol to request and receive these segments, which are then stitched together to create the seamless playback of your video.

The HLS approach has some important advantages: first, as we've mentioned, the video can be stored and delivered from any conventional web server. Also, given the pervasiveness of the HTTP protocol, many of the potential network issues we encounter with proprietary protocols

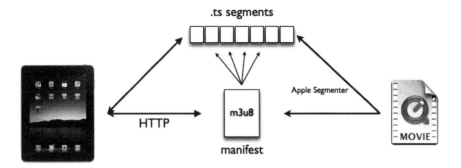

.ts segments

Apple Segmenter

HTTP

m3u8

manifest

MOVIE

Figure 9.1: APPLE HTTP LIVE STREAMING

with routers and firewalls are avoided. There is also another significant advantage: because the video is broken into segments, each time the player needs to fetch a new segment, it can make a decision about the available bandwidth and, if available, request a segment that has been encoded at a greater or lesser bit rate, improving the quality of service of the video delivery.

Segmenting Video

As you might expect, segmenting video introduces some extra work because it requires preprocessing your video into small chunks (typically ten seconds in length) to be used by HLS, and further, in order to use the bit rate shifting, you'll need to do this several times for the same asset (once for each bit rate you want to support).

Segmenting video is beyond the scope of this book; however, there are many Apple tools and resources to help. Check out the *HTTP Live Streaming Overview* [App09a], which itself contains pointers to all the tools and background you'll need to prepare your video for HLS. Although we aren't going to cover segmenting in detail, you do need to have some knowledge of the output of the Apple's segmenter tool to understand how the client retrieves video from a web server.

The segmenter process is depicted in Figure 9.1, on the preceding page —here the segmenter takes a video asset and produces a set of .ts files (the segments) along with a manifest file (sometimes called a *playlist*— not to be confused with the playlists we implemented in Chapter 7, *The Movie Player*, on page 121). HLS's manifest files are called M3U8 files, and here's an example:

```
#EXTM3U
#EXT-X-TARGETDURATION:10
#EXT-X-MEDIA-SEQUENCE:0
#EXTINF:10, no desc
fileSequence0.ts
#EXTINF:10, no desc
fileSequence1.ts
#EXTINF:10, no desc
fileSequence2.ts
#EXTINF:10, no desc
fileSequence3.ts
.
.
.
#EXTINF:1, no desc
fileSequence180.ts
#EXT-X-ENDLIST
```

The job of the manifest file is to describe every video segment that was generated from a given video asset (the usage is slightly different in live video applications, which are beyond the scope of our discussion here).

Let's step through the file. The first line identifies the file's type. The next line, the target duration, describes how long each segment is (in this case ten seconds), while the third line provides a sequence number that is used for live streaming applications. Next, each segment is listed in order (for space, we've omitted some of the 180 sequences), including its duration, an optional description, and finally the asset name for the segment.

So, given this playlist, the media player first retrieves fileSequence0.ts followed by fileSequence1.ts, and so on. The player itself manages all the timing aspects of when to retrieve the segments and how to stitch them together to make the playback seamless.

Now, a manifest file like the previous one would typically be generated for each bit rate we're going to support. So, we need another file to describe all the possible segments (by bit rate) that are available. That file looks like this:

```
#EXTM3U
#EXT-X-STREAM-INF:PROGRAM-ID=1, BANDWIDTH=200000
gear1/prog_index.m3u8
#EXT-X-STREAM-INF:PROGRAM-ID=1, BANDWIDTH=311111
gear2/prog_index.m3u8
#EXT-X-STREAM-INF:PROGRAM-ID=1, BANDWIDTH=484444
gear3/prog_index.m3u8
#EXT-X-STREAM-INF:PROGRAM-ID=1, BANDWIDTH=737777
gear4/prog_index.m3u8
```

This M3U8 file lists four possible assets, one encoded at 200Kbps and available in the gear1/prog_index.m3u8 manifest file, another available at 311Kbps and available in the gear2/prog_index.m3u8 file, and so on. When you point a player to this file, the player will parse it to determine each available bit rate so it can make decisions about which asset to retrieve next based on available bandwidth. Note when your player first retrieves content, it will always start with the first listed manifest file and then judge its later retrievals based on network conditions.

Taking HLS Further

As you may suspect, we've barely scratched the surface of segmenting and configuration of the back end of HLS, and if you're serious about using HLS, there is a lot to learn. That said, CDN and other vendors will also gladly take most of the pain away from you if you want them to host your HLS content.

For now, with a basic understanding of segmenting, we're going to move on to the real topic of this chapter: how to support streaming on the client side.

9.3 Creating a Streaming Player

As you're going to see, getting a streaming player up and running is quite easy given all the work you've done over the past two chapters. We're going to go back to MoviePlayer3 and start there—actually, we've created a new version of this called MoviePlayer3Streamed.

We're going to ask you to make one small change to the file MoviePlayerViewController.m: locate the movieURL method, delete all the code in it, and then replace the code with this:

`movieplayer/MoviePlayer3Streamed/Classes/MoviePlayerViewController.m`

```
-(NSURL *)movieURL
{
 return [NSURL URLWithString:
   @"http://devimages.apple.com/iphone/samples/bipbop/gear1/prog_index.m3u8"];
}
```

Before we talk about this new code, note that the code you just deleted created an NSURL that pointed to a resource in the bundle; here, instead, you're creating a URL that points to an M3U8 file hosted on Apple's servers.

Make this change, compile, and run (making sure you are network connected first). You should see, after a bit of buffering, a test video like the one in Figure 9.2, on the facing page. Note this video is at a fairly low bit rate (by observing the video quality).

Now, make this quick change; change the URL to the following:

```
http://devimages.apple.com/iphone/samples/bipbop/gear2/prog_index.m3u8
```

A little better quality? (We're assuming you have the bandwidth to stream it.) Let's try one more time; use this URL:

```
http://devimages.apple.com/iphone/samples/bipbop/gear4/prog_index.m3u8
```

Even better? OK, now we're going to point the player to an M3U8 file that points to all of these, and the player can decide which is best:

```
http://devimages.apple.com/iphone/samples/bipbop/bipbopall.m3u8
```

This time, you should see the stream start with the lowest-quality stream, and after ten seconds, you may see it adjust. Assuming you have a lot of bandwidth, you'll most likely see the highest-resolution version after ten seconds (or more, if the player has managed to buffer more content).

9.4 Reacting to a Network Environment

One nice feature of Apple's implementation is that it handles all the details of performing bit rate changes as the network conditions change. That said, you'll still encounter times when the network bandwidth isn't sufficient, causing the video playback to stall. When that

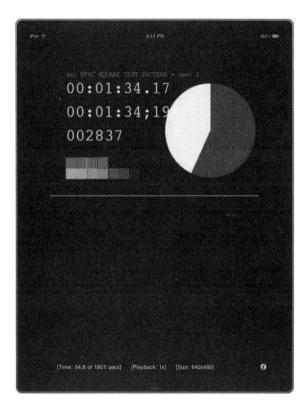

Figure 9.2: A STREAMING TEST PATTERN

happens, you can use the MPMoviePlayerLoadStateDidChangeNotification notification to provide an application-specific behavior. Let's add a bit of code to experiment with this: first register to receive the notification from your viewDidLoad method, and specify handleLoadStateDidChange: as the selector.

movieplayer/MoviePlayer3Streamed/Classes/MoviePlayerViewController.m

```
[[NSNotificationCenter defaultCenter]
 addObserver:self
 selector:@selector(handleLoadStateDidChange:)
 name:MPMoviePlayerLoadStateDidChangeNotification
 object:nil];
```

Now before defining the handleLoadStateDidChange method, you're going to add a UIActivityIndicatorView to the MoviePlayerViewController.xib nib. Drag an UIActivityIndicatorView onto the main nib view; we set ours to a style of Large White and also clicked "Hide when stopped." Also add

How Do I Know Which Bit Rate the Player Is Playing?

Unfortunately, Apple does not expose any method of determining the bit rate it is currently playing. After you've set the player's content URL to an M3U8 file, the player handles all the logic and provides no feedback in terms of switching between the available streams. You can, however, be notified when the load of content changes in some way (such as a video stall); we cover that in Section 9.4, *Reacting to a Network Environment*, on page 174.

an IBOutlet to MoviePlayerViewController.h, and name it activityView; then, connect it in Interface Builder.

With that in place, it's almost time to define the handleLoadStateDidChange: method. First, though, we need to know a little more about load states. The load states are defined as an enum and include the following:

MPMovieLoadStateUnknown
> The load state is not known.

MPMovieLoadStatePlayable
> The player is in a state where video can be played, but it may run out of buffer.

MPMovieLoadStatePlaythroughOK
> The player is ready to play with enough buffer to begin playback.

MPMovieLoadStateStalled
> The player has stalled.

OK, now let's define handleLoadStateDidChange:

movieplayer/MoviePlayer3Streamed/Classes/MoviePlayerViewController.m

```
- (void) handleLoadStateDidChange:(NSNotification*)notification {
        MPMovieLoadState state = [player loadState];

        if (state & MPMovieLoadStateStalled) {
                [activityView startAnimating];
        } else if (state & MPMovieLoadStatePlaythroughOK) {
                [activityView stopAnimating];
        }
}
```

Here we first obtain the load state from the player. We are interested in two states, MPMovieLoadStateStalled and MPMovieLoadStatePlaythrough-OK). In the case where the load state is MPMovieLoadStateStalled, we want to start the activity indicator animating because the video is stalled, and we want to indicate to the user there is some buffer activity occurring in the background. Likewise, when the state is MPMovieLoadStatePlay-throughOK), we want to stop the animation of the indicator because the video is once again playing.

Enter this code, and compile and run it. Testing may be tricky because you will have to simulate an unreliable network connection. You can often do this by temporarily disconnecting your Ethernet (from your wireless router, or if you're using the simulator, from your Macintosh).

That's it! You've now walked through all the basic details of streaming content on the client side.

9.5 Summary

We've just walked through the basics of video streaming, which, combined with all the tools we've covered in the two previous chapters, will give you a huge head start in creating compelling video-based experiences. That's not to say we've covered every detail; in particular, there are many aspects of streaming, such as being able to switch streams in the middle of playback (say, for ad serving), that you'll need to dive into the details of segmenting and the HLS protocol to achieve. You should also note that HLS is a young protocol, and it and the corresponding implementation in the MPMoviePlayerController are sure to grow and change over the next several versions.

Chapter 10

Displaying Content on Another Screen

Apple provides a set of adapter cables, such as the iPad Dock Connector to VGA Adapter (composite and component versions are also available), that allow you to connect your iPad to an external screen, such as a large projector or monitor. Now, you might expect, particularly after seeing Steve Jobs demo the iPad in his keynotes, that this adapter is used to mirror your iPad's main screen on an external screen. That's not the case, and unfortunately, whatever Steve is using to mirror his iPad, it isn't available to the rest of us. That said, for many applications, mirroring the display isn't the best option anyway; for instance, consider a presentation application where you want the audience to view your slides on the external screen while you're looking at a set of notes on the main screen.

In this chapter, you're going to learn how to integrate a secondary screen into your applications. To do that, you need to understand how to detect the second screen, how to get a reference to its screen object, and how to create views on it. You'll also need to consider how you want to use this second screen (and also remember it isn't a Multi-Touch display that the user is directly interacting with). We're going to start with a simple application that looks for an external display and then build from there, all the way to displaying full-screen video.

Figure 10.1: SETTING UP A STATUS LABEL

10.1 Detecting an External Display

To display content on an external monitor, you first need to know whether a second screen is connected to the iPad. The UIScreen class provides two notifications, UIScreenDidConnectNotification and UIScreenDidDisconnectNotification, that are posted when a new screen is connected or disconnected from the iPad. Let's create a simple view-based application that can detect when we plug or unplug an external screen.

Start by creating a new view-based application in Xcode called ExternalDisplay. Next, open the ExternalDisplayViewController.xib nib, and add two labels, as shown in Figure 10.1. Then add an outlet to the ExternalDisplayViewController.h header file named statusLabel, and connect it in Interface Builder to the status label (the label on the right side).

Now open the ExternalDisplayViewController class, uncomment the supplied viewDidLoad method, and add the following code to register to receive both of the UIScreen notifications:

ExternalDisplay/ExternalDisplay1/Classes/ExternalDisplayViewController.m

```
- (void)viewDidLoad {
    [super viewDidLoad];

        NSNotificationCenter *notificationCenter =
        [NSNotificationCenter defaultCenter];
```

```
▶         [notificationCenter addObserver:self
▶                 selector:@selector(screenDidConnectNotification:)
▶                 name:UIScreenDidConnectNotification
▶                 object:nil];
▶         [notificationCenter addObserver:self
▶                 selector:@selector(screenDidDisconnectNotification:)
▶                 name:UIScreenDidDisconnectNotification
▶                 object:nil];
    }
```

Here we obtain a reference to the NSNotificationCenter and use it to register for the UIScreenDidConnectNotification notification, which, when posted, results in the screenDidConnectNotification: method being called; and likewise, the UIScreenDidDisconnectNotification, when posted, results in the screenDidDisconnectNotification: method being called.

Let's write these two methods now:

ExternalDisplay/ExternalDisplay1/Classes/ExternalDisplayViewController.m

```
- (void)screenDidConnectNotification:(NSNotification *)notification {
      statusLabel.text = @"Connected";
}
```

ExternalDisplay/ExternalDisplay1/Classes/ExternalDisplayViewController.m

```
- (void)screenDidDisconnectNotification:(NSNotification *)notification {
      statusLabel.text = @"Not Connected";
}
```

There's not a lot going on here; we're just updating the status of the statusLabel as the external screen is connected and disconnected. One thing we should point out for future reference is that the UIScreenDid-ConnectNotification notification's object will point to the newly attached UIScreen object. So, we can get access the new UIScreen object like this:

```
UIScreen *externalScreen = (UIScreen *)[notification object];
```

We'll come back and use this in a bit. At this point, you're ready to give this code a try: build and install the code on your iPad, and then unplug your device from your development machine (doing so will cause the application to quit if it is running on the device). Now, touch the application icon to restart it, and then plug and unplug the adapter cable; you'll see the status label change as you do.

With that now working, think about this: what happens when you launch your application and an external screen is already connected? No notification will be sent during or after the start of your application (at least until someone unplugs the cable), so the status is going to display "Not Connected" when it should read "Connected."

To handle that, we're going to need to do a manual check when we start the application to see whether a second screen is attached. How? We're going to do it through the UIScreen class, which provides two class methods we're going to use: screens and mainScreen. The mainScreen method returns the UIScreen object that represents the main display of the device. The screens method, on the other hand, returns an array of UIScreen objects, one for each connected display. With the iPad, there can be only one external screen attached given the currently available connectors,[1] so given that, let's write some code to determine whether there is a second screen and, if so, return its UIScreen object:

ExternalDisplay/ExternalDisplay1/Classes/ExternalDisplayViewController.m

```
-(UIScreen *)scanForExternalScreen {
        NSArray *deviceScreens = [UIScreen screens];
        for (UIScreen *screen in deviceScreens) {
                if (![screen isEqual:[UIScreen mainScreen]]) {
                        return screen;
                }
        }
        return nil;
}
```

Here we're first making use of the screens class method, which returns an array of the connected screens. On the iPad, if there is no external screen, this will be an array with a size of one with its only element being a reference to the main screen. If there is a connected screen, then this will be an array of size two.

We then iterate through the array, looking for a screen that isn't the main screen—our comparison is done with the screen that is returned from the mainScreen class method. If we find a screen that isn't the main screen, we immediately return it. If we don't find one, we return nil.

Now that we have this method, we can use it at application launch to determine the correct status for the statusLabel (connected or disconnected). You'll want to first add a property to your ExternalDisplayViewController class of type UIScreen called externalScreen to hold a reference to the display. Next, add this code to your viewDidLoad method:

ExternalDisplay/ExternalDisplay1/Classes/ExternalDisplayViewController.m

```
externalScreen = [self scanForExternalScreen];
if (externalScreen) {
        statusLabel.text = @"Connected";
}
```

---

1. Obviously, this could change after the printing of this book.

Now, when we launch the application, the viewDidLoad: method checks to see whether there is a display already connected and, if so, sets the status label to Connected.

Before we move on, let's improve the screenDidConnectNotification: method by also setting the externalScreen property when we're notified a screen is attached—remember, we mentioned earlier that the object of the UIScreenDidConnectNotification notification contains the UIScreen object of the newly attached screen. Given that we can capture the external screen like this:

ExternalDisplay/ExternalDisplay1/Classes/ExternalDisplayViewController.m

```
- (void)screenDidConnectNotification:(NSNotification *)notification {
        statusLabel.text = @"Connected";
        externalScreen = (UIScreen *)[notification object];
}
```

add this code to your screenDidConnectNotification: method, and test the code by trying various states of having the iPad plugged in.

10.2 Simple Output to the External Display

Now that we know when an external display is connected, we can start using it. We're going to begin by creating a window/view hierarchy on the external screen and using it to set the screen's color. First, on the iPad's main display, let's create a color chooser (actually, let's just reuse the one we made in Chapter 4, *Popovers and Modal Dialog Boxes*, on page 75). To do that, start by opening the ExternalDisplay/ExternalDisplay2/ExternalDisplay.xcodeproj project, and you'll find we have already added the cargo color chooser from Chapter 4, *Popovers and Modal Dialog Boxes*, on page 75:

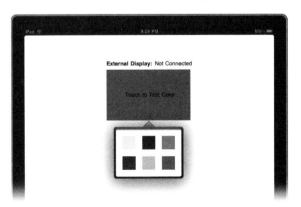

We also wired everything together so that when a color is chosen, the color view is updated in the setbackgroundColor: method:

ExternalDisplay/ExternalDisplay2/Classes/ExternalDisplayViewController.m

```
-(void)setbackgroundColor:(UIColor *)theColor {
        colorView.backgroundColor = theColor;
}
```

Now what we need is a view on the external display so that we can set its background color. Let's do that like this:

ExternalDisplay/ExternalDisplay2/Classes/ExternalDisplayViewController.m

```
-(void)setupExternalScreen {
        if (!externalScreen) {
                externalScreen = [self scanForExternalScreen];
        }

        if (externalScreen) {
                statusLabel.text = @"Connected";
                UIWindow *thisWindow = [[UIWindow alloc]
                        initWithFrame:[externalScreen bounds]];
                [thisWindow setScreen:externalScreen];
                externalView = [[UIView alloc]
                        initWithFrame:[thisWindow bounds]];
                [externalView setBackgroundColor:[UIColor grayColor]];
                [thisWindow addSubview:externalView];
                [thisWindow makeKeyAndVisible];
        }
}
```

Here we've created a new method to handle the specifics of setting up a new view hierarchy. Let's walk through this method: first, we make sure there is an external screen; if there isn't, we scan for one. If we find one, then we make sure our status label is set correctly, and we begin creating the view.

Once we have our hands on the screen object, we need a UIWindow to place our view in. Given that, we next instantiate a UIWindow object and set its screen property. We also set its frame to match the bounds of the screen.[2] We then create a UIView and base its bounds on the window's. Finally, we set the view to a background color of gray, add it as a subview, and make the entire window visible. Note that the UIView

---

2. If you'd like to use another supported size for your external display, you can use the UIScreen's availableModes property to introspect the support modes of the screen object. You can then set the currentModes property to the mode you'd like.

> **<u>My iPad Doesn't Always See the Screen When I Unplug and Plug Back In</u>**
>
> Plugging and unplugging while your app is running appears to be unreliable across developer applications (as well as with some of the built-in applications, such as YouTube). That said, restarting the app usually solves any issues.

object is assigned to a property, called externalView; you'll need to add this property to your header file.

Enter this code. Now, to use the code, you'll want to add a call to the setupExternalScreen: method in your viewDidLoad: method, like this:

```
[self setupExternalScreen];
```

You'll also need to add code to your screenDidConnectNotification: method so that when the iPad is connected to a display, it creates the window and view (add this code to the bottom of your method):

ExternalDisplay/ExternalDisplay2/Classes/ExternalDisplayViewController.m

```
if (externalScreen == nil) {
        [self setupExternalScreen];
}
```

After you've made these changes, run the application, and you should now see a gray screen when you connect the external screen to your iPad.

Let's get color working. After all this work, doing so is straightforward: just add this to your setbackgroundColor: method:

ExternalDisplay/ExternalDisplay2/Classes/ExternalDisplayViewController.m

```
-(void)setbackgroundColor:(UIColor *)theColor {
        colorView.backgroundColor = theColor;
        if (externalScreen) {
                [externalView setBackgroundColor:theColor];
        }
}
```

Add this code, and give the application a spin.

You should be able to set your screen to all the following colors:

Adding Views to the External Display

Now that we have a window object on the external display, we can create any views we choose; just remember the user has no means of interacting directly with the screen. For instance, we can easily add a nice watermark logo to the screen by adding a UIImageView:

ExternalDisplay/ExternalDisplay2/Classes/ExternalDisplayViewController.m

```objc
-(void)setupExternalScreen {
        if (!externalScreen) {
                externalScreen = [self scanForExternalScreen];
        }

        if (externalScreen) {
                statusLabel.text = @"Connected";
                UIWindow *thisWindow = [[UIWindow alloc]
                        initWithFrame:[externalScreen bounds]];
                [thisWindow setScreen:externalScreen];
                externalView = [[UIView alloc]
                        initWithFrame:[thisWindow bounds]];
                [externalView setBackgroundColor:[UIColor grayColor]];
                [thisWindow addSubview:externalView];
                [thisWindow makeKeyAndVisible];

►               CGRect rect = [externalScreen bounds];
►               rect.origin.x = (rect.size.width - 500) / 2;
►               rect.origin.y = (rect.size.height - 300) / 2;
►               rect.size.width = 500;
►               rect.size.height = 300;
►
►               UIImageView *imageView =
►               [[UIImageView alloc] initWithFrame:rect];
►               [imageView setImage:[UIImage imageNamed:@"logo.png"]];
►               imageView.frame = rect;
►
►               [externalView addSubview:imageView];
        }
}
```

Here, we're just obtaining the bounds of the screen and then centering the logo.png within the UIView. This is how our version looks:

10.3 Sending Video Content to the External Display

What's better to display on a (potentially large) external screen than video? Sound difficult? Well, we have everything we need in place to make it happen (especially if we borrow some code from Chapter 7, *The Movie Player*, on page 121).

Open the ExternalDisplay/ExternalDisplay3/ExternalDisplay.xcodeproj project, and you'll see we have everything ready for you. Open the ExternalDisplayViewController.xib nib, and you'll see we've added a small view along with a Switch Screen button:

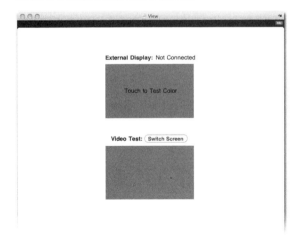

Before we add any code, build the application; you should see video begin playing on the iPad, as depicted on the next page.[3]

---

3. Refer to Chapter 7, *The Movie Player*, on page 121, to find out how to acquire this video, or substitute your own video.

Our challenge is now to enable the Switch button so that by touching it, the user can switch the display back and forth between the two screens. We've already set up the button's action to be the switchMovie method; now we just need to define this method. Let's give this is a little thought before jumping into it: what we need to do is determine where the video is playing (on the main stream or on the external screen) and then switch the video to the other screen. How do we do that? Well, you might remember from Chapter 7, *The Movie Player*, on page 121 that the way the MPMovieViewController works is that we supply it with a view, and it displays its video on that view. So, we can check to see whether the movie player's view is currently our view on the iPad main stream or on the external screen and then handle the logistics of switching them. Let's give this a try:

ExternalDisplay/ExternalDisplay3/Classes/ExternalDisplayViewController.m

```
-(IBAction)switchMovie {
        if (player.view.superview == viewForMovie) {
                [player.view removeFromSuperview];
                [externalView addSubview:player.view];
        } else {
                [player.view removeFromSuperview];
                [viewForMovie addSubview:player.view];
        }
}
```

Here, as we discussed, we're checking the player.view property and seeing whether it is the iPad's main stream view, that is, viewForMovie; if it is, we remove that view from the player and use the external view. If the video is playing on the external screen, we remove that view and set the player's view to viewForMovie on the iPad's main screen. Add that code, and then compile and give the code a try.

Well, that wasn't bad for a first try; the video switches back and forth between each screen as we'd expect. However, we have a little polishing to do—if you're seeing what we're seeing, the video's size isn't scaling up to the external display. Let's put the external display in full-screen mode when we switch:

ExternalDisplay/ExternalDisplay3/Classes/ExternalDisplayViewController.m
```
-(IBAction)switchMovie {
        if (player.view.superview == viewForMovie) {
                [player.view removeFromSuperview];
                [externalView addSubview:player.view];
                [player setFullscreen:YES animated:NO];
        } else {
                [player.view removeFromSuperview];
                [viewForMovie addSubview:player.view];
                [player setFullscreen:NO animated:NO];
        }
}
```

Now compile and give it a try—ah, exactly what we were looking for: when we switch to the external display, we see full-screen video. Nice!

10.4 Summary

In this chapter, you've seen there's a small bit of work you need to do to keep track of a second screen, and beyond that, placing content on an external view is just a matter of creating views as we do on the main screen. Of course, we have to keep in mind that the second screen isn't a Multi-Touch device (at least not yet), and we often want to handle the second screen as a different type of display than our main screen.

Although we won't be able to easily mirror the main screen on an external screen until Apple gives us that ability, it isn't clear that that is often what we want anyway. For now, we have enough tools to create some really interesting applications that use the second screen if it's present.

Chapter 11

Connecting Devices

The iPad has a big enough screen that you could easily play all sorts of board games on it. You could play Chess, Go, Backgammon, and so on. You couldn't play a game where it's important that players not see the cards that another is holding. That eliminates games such as Mastermind, Scrabble, Battleship, and most competitive card games.[1]

Or does it?

What if we didn't just use one iPad for game play? What if we used more than one iPad or one iPad as the common board and iPhones and iPod touches to hold the items we need to hide from other players?[2] It seems kind of silly to use thousands of dollars of devices to replace a two-dollar deck of cards, but start to think about what changes when groups of people have compatible devices. What new kinds of experiences can you create for multiple connected devices that don't quite make sense for a solo device? As you build your app, you should consider ways in which it can become more powerful if it could find other instances of the app running nearby.

In this chapter, we'll look at two simple examples that demonstrate different techniques you'll use to communicate between your iPad and a second device. In the first example, we'll create a server and client network to implement a classic problem known as the Monty Hall problem. In the second example, we'll implement a simple peer-to-peer chat system that demonstrates a different way of discovering and connecting to

---

1. The rights to Mastermind are held by Invicta Plastics, the Scrabble rights are held by Hasbro, and the Battleship rights are held by Milton Bradley Company.
2. You'll already find examples on the App Store of these multidevice apps for all sorts of games and for more serious applications.

peers on a network. Both examples use Apple's Game Kit framework and run over Bluetooth to work with devices that are within meters of each other.

11.1 The Monty Hall Problem

For our first example, we'll use a puzzle based on the old television game show *Let's Make a Deal*. The puzzle is named for the show's long-time host, Monty Hall. In the puzzle there are three doors. Behind one of them is a desirable prize of some sort, and behind the other two there is nothing of value. The contestant chooses a door. The host then opens one of the doors the contestant didn't select to show that there's nothing of value behind it. The host then gives the contestant the choice of keeping their original door or switching. The puzzle is whether the contestant should switch or whether it doesn't make any difference.[3]

We're going to create two distinct applications. One will present the game from the contestant's point of view, and the other will present the game from the game show host's point of view. We could also have created a single application that has the ability to be either the host or the contestant. In our case, the roles are so distinctive that it makes sense for one application to act as the server and the other as a client. It wouldn't make sense for two contestants to find each other or for two hosts to find each other. On the other hand, if you were coding up a card game, it might make more sense for the players to be peers.

You'll find our two applications in the code download. One is called Contestant. It is a view-based iPad application. The other is called MontyHall. We've decided to create it as a view-based iPhone application because many developers don't have two iPads but do have an iPad and either an iPhone or an iPod touch.[4]

We are using Game Kit to communicate between our two devices, so you will need to push each application to its respective device. Also, based on personal experience, you will be much happier with the results if you make sure that Bluetooth is enabled in both devices. You'll need to do this in Settings.

---

3. The solution is that the contestant should always switch. Playing the role of the host in this two-person game should help convince you of that.
4. We could, of course, have created a universal application for both, but we wanted to keep the code focused on what is being taught here. Of course, you can connect multiple iPads, iPhones, or a mixture of the two.

11.2 Launching and Advertising the Server

The Contestant application will act as the server. When the view controller loads the view, it will create a GKSession object, set the view controller as the session delegate, and announce that the session is now available using the initWithSessionID:displayName:sessionMode: method.[5]

The initWithSessionID:displayName:sessionMode: method takes three parameters. The first is a Bonjour-style service name. You should register your name with the DNS-SD registry (http://www.dns-sd.org/ServiceTypes.html). We are using example as our service name because that has been reserved specifically to be used by books for their examples.

The second parameter is where you pass in a friendly name that others can use to recognize you. In this case, we're hard-coding it as Contestant, but often you'll let the user enter a name that will be used.

The final parameter is where you specify the mode of the session you are launching. You can be a server and advertise the session for others to find, a client and search for advertised sessions, or a peer and both advertise sessions and search for those advertised by others.[6]

We'll initialize the session in this launchServerSession method which we invoke in the viewDidLoad method.

```
Devices/Contestant1/Classes/ContestantViewController.m
-(void)launchServerSession {
    self.session = [[GKSession alloc] initWithSessionID:@"example"
                                           displayName:@"Contestant"
                                           sessionMode:GKSessionModeServer];

    self.session.delegate = self;
    self.session.available = YES;
}
```

Once you have advertised the new session, there's little more you can do but wait. In other words, you'll implement the appropriate delegate methods, and these methods will be called when there is a change the host needs to respond to. The host will need to respond when it receives a connection request and when it detects that another device has successfully connected to it or has been disconnected from it.

---

5. Remember, of course, to declare the GKSessionDelegate protocol in ContestantViewController.h.

6. The terminology is a bit confusing because once you are connected to a session, you will refer to all of the other devices you are connected to as your peers regardless of how they connect to the session.

To begin with, we'll respond when a client requests a connection by implementing the session:didRecieveConnectionRequestFromPeer: method like this:

Devices/Contestant1/Classes/ContestantViewController.m

```
- (void)session:(GKSession *)session
didReceiveConnectionRequestFromPeer:(NSString *)peerID {
    self.statusField.text =
        [NSString stringWithFormat:@"%@ has asked to be our host.",
                        [self.session displayNameForPeer:peerID]];
    NSError *error1;
    [self.session acceptConnectionFromPeer:peerID error:&error1];
}
```

In a fussier application, you might display a modal view with a message allowing your user to determine whether to accept this request. In our case, we're going to accept any request. We do that in the message to the GKSession object passed in as a parameter to acceptConnectionFromPeer:.

Whenever you program an application where devices communicate over a network somehow, you must account for the fact that devices come and go. We will watch for these changes by implementing the method session:peer:didChangeState: so that we are notified when a peer becomes connected or disconnected.

Devices/Contestant1/Classes/ContestantViewController.m

```
- (void)session:(GKSession *)session
            peer:(NSString *)peerID
 didChangeState:(GKPeerConnectionState)state {
    switch (state) {
        case GKPeerStateConnected:
            [self connectToPeer:peerID];
            break;
        case GKPeerStateDisconnected:
            self.statusField.text = @"The host has disconnected.";
            //put actual handling code here
            break;
        default:
            break;
    }

}
```

When we get connected to a client, we call a method named connect-ToPeer: so that we can isolate what we do when we are notified of a connection in its own method. In connectToPeer:, we will display a message saying we're connected and set our session to no longer be available so that no more clients can connect to it. We'll also use the setDataReceiveHandler: method to tell the session which object is responsible for handling data sent to our peer. In our case, we'll let the view controller take care of any data we get.

`Devices/Contestant1/Classes/ContestantViewController.m`

```objc
-(void)connectToPeer:(NSString *) peerID{
    self.statusField.text = [NSString stringWithFormat: @"%@ is our host.",
                            [self.session displayNameForPeer:peerID]];
    self.session.available = NO;
    [self.session setDataReceiveHandler:self withContext:nil];
}
```

Before we implement any more of the server, let's see what it takes to launch the client and find this server.

11.3 Launching and Connecting the Client

The code used to launch the client is almost identical to what we used to launch the server. This time, the mode is set to GKSessionModeClient.

`Devices/MontyHall1/Classes/MontyHallViewController.m`

```objc
-(void) launchClientSession {
    self.session = [[GKSession alloc] initWithSessionID:@"example"
                                    displayName:@"Monty"
                                    sessionMode:GKSessionModeClient];
    self.session.delegate = self;
    self.session.available = YES;
}
```

You'll again implement the session:peer:didChangeState: delegate method to respond to different changes in state by discovered peers. In this case, we'll respond to finding an available peer, connecting to the peer, and disconnecting from the peer.

`Devices/MontyHall1/Classes/MontyHallViewController.m`

```objc
- (void)session:(GKSession *)session
         peer:(NSString *)peerID
 didChangeState:(GKPeerConnectionState)state {
    switch (state) {
        case GKPeerStateAvailable:
            [self connectToAvailablePeer:peerID];
            break;
        case GKPeerStateConnected:
            [self beginSession];
            break;
        case GKPeerStateDisconnected:
            //handle services disconnecting
            break;
```

```
        default:
            break;
    }
}
```

When we discover an available peer, we attempt to connect to it. We create the connectToAvailablePeer: that we call in case the connection state is GKPeerStateAvailable. In this method, we will update the message we're displaying and call the connectToPeer:withTimeout: method to attempt to connect to the discovered device.

Devices/MontyHall1/Classes/MontyHallViewController.m

```
-(void) connectToAvailablePeer:(NSString *) peerID {
    self.statusField.text = [NSString stringWithFormat: @"Connecting to %@.",
                            [self.session displayNameForPeer:peerID]];
    [self.session connectToPeer:peerID withTimeout:3000];
}
```

When the device, known to our application as a peer, reports that its state has changed to GKPeerStateConnected, we call our beginSession method. In it, we send a message to the user to start playing the game, and we mark the session as no longer being available.

Devices/MontyHall1/Classes/MontyHallViewController.m

```
-(void) beginSession {
    self.statusField.text = @"Pick a door to place the prize.";
    self.session.available = NO;
}
```

If you run both the MontyHall and the Contestant applications on different iOS devices that have Bluetooth turned on, you should see the devices find each other and begin the session.

11.4 Adding Some Game Logic

We'll implement our game show host to have a button for each of the doors. Set up outlets named door1, door2, and door3 for the doors, and declare an action named selectDoor: that all of the buttons call when pressed. We'll also add a property of type NSArray named doors to hold these doors.

When we begin the session, we'll build an array named doors that consists of the three buttons, we'll unhide the buttons, and we'll set the view controller to receive any data sent by the contestant.

```
-(void) beginSession {
    self.statusField.text = @"Pick a door to place the prize.";
    self.session.available = NO;
►   self.doors = [NSArray arrayWithObjects:self.door1, self.door2,
►                                          self.door3, nil];
►   [self setAllDoorsToHidden:NO];
►   [self.session setDataReceiveHandler:self withContext:nil];
►   [door1 release];
►   [door2 release];
►   [door3 release];
}
```

The view controller waits for the user to pick a door. There are two different times in the game life cycle when a door can be selected. This first time we are selecting the door behind which we are hiding the prize, so the isPrizeInPlace has value NO. If you look at our action, you'll see that our first time through we'll call the placePrizeBehindDoor: method.

```
-(IBAction) selectDoor:(id)sender {
    if (isPrizeInPlace) {
        [self revealDoor:sender];
    } else {
        [self placePrizeBehindDoor:sender];
    }
}
```

The placePrizeBehindDoor: method disables the buttons so that the game show host can't make further changes, displays a message, and turns the selected door number green and the other two numbers red. You can also see that we store the number of the door that was selected, and we change the isPrizeInPlace flag so the revealDoor: method will be called the next time a button is pressed.

```
-(void) placePrizeBehindDoor:(id)sender {
    [self setAllDoorsToEnabled:NO];
    self.statusField.text = @"Wait while contestant makes their choice.";
    prizeDoor = ((UIButton *)sender).tag;
    [self setAllDoorsRedExcept:(UIButton *)sender];
    [self sendMessage:@"hideThePrize:" forDoor:prizeDoor];
    isPrizeInPlace = YES;
}
```

If the third door was selected, our interface looks something like this:

There's one other important action performed in the placePrizeBehind-Door: method. The sendMessage:forDoor: message is sent. This is what initiates sending the information about which door was chosen to the connected device.

11.5 Sending Data to Another Device

Whatever we send from one device to another needs to be wrapped up as NSData. In our sendMessage:forDoor: method, we prepare the data to be sent by creating a keyed archive with the key equal to the method name to be called at the other end and the value equal to the door number. We will then send the information to the contestant using this call:

Devices/MontyHall2/Classes/MontyHallViewController.m

```
[self.session sendDataToAllPeers:data
                withDataMode:GKSendDataReliable
                     error:&error2];
```

We could send the data to all peers or to a specific peer. We're sending it to all peers because we have only one peer, so there's no sense in narrowing it down. We can specify whether we need the data to be sent reliably. We've chosen GKSendDataReliable so it will be sent until the send is successful or until the connection times out.

Putting this together with the archiving of the data and the memory management, here's our sendMessage:forDoor: method:

Devices/MontyHall2/Classes/MontyHallViewController.m

```
-(void) sendMessage:(NSString *)message
          forDoor:(NSUInteger) doorNumber {
   NSMutableData *data = [[NSMutableData alloc] init];
   NSKeyedArchiver *archiver =
     [[NSKeyedArchiver alloc] initForWritingWithMutableData:data];
   [archiver encodeInt:doorNumber forKey:message];
   [archiver finishEncoding];
   NSError *error2;
   [self.session sendDataToAllPeers:data
                     withDataMode:GKSendDataReliable
                            error:&error2];
   [archiver release];
   [data release];
}
```

With that, the data is sent to all peers. Next, let's see what the contestant does when it receives the message.

11.6 Receiving Data Sent from Another Device

Remember, we registered the ContestantViewController object as being interested in data sent to the session with this call:

Devices/Contestant2/Classes/ContestantViewController.m

```
[self.session setDataReceiveHandler:self withContext:nil];
```

When your session receives data, the system calls the delegate message named receiveData:fromPeer:inSession:context:. We'll unarchive the data and look to see which key was sent for the data. We'll call the method with that name and send the door number as its argument.

Devices/Contestant2/Classes/ContestantViewController.m

```
- (void) receiveData: (NSData*) data
        fromPeer: (NSString*) peerID
            inSession: (GKSession*) session
          context: (void*) context {
   NSKeyedUnarchiver *unarchiver =
   [[NSKeyedUnarchiver alloc] initForReadingWithData:data];
   if ([unarchiver containsValueForKey:@"hideThePrize:"]) {
      [self hideThePrize: [unarchiver decodeIntForKey:@"hideThePrize:"]];
   } else if ([unarchiver containsValueForKey:@"revealAnEmptyDoor:"]) {
      [self revealAnEmptyDoor:
                   [unarchiver decodeIntForKey:@"revealAnEmptyDoor:"]];
   }
}
```

In our case, we're calling the hideThePrize: method. There's nothing particularly interesting about what that method does. But at some point the Contestant user is able to choose a door and that gets bundled up and sent back to the MontyHall application.

Just to illustrate a different approach, we'll use a slightly different strategy to receive the data in the MontyHall app. This time we're eliminating some of the repetition from the receiveData:fromPeer:inSession:context: method:

Devices/MontyHall2/Classes/MontyHallViewController.m
```
- (void) receiveData: (NSData*) data
          fromPeer: (NSString*) peerID
         inSession: (GKSession*) session
           context: (void*) context {
    NSKeyedUnarchiver *unarchiver =
    [[NSKeyedUnarchiver alloc] initForReadingWithData:data];
    [self invokeMethodForKey:@"contestantDidChooseDoor:" ifFoundIn:unarchiver];
    [self invokeMethodForKey:@"finalDoorSelected:" ifFoundIn:unarchiver];
}
```

The invokeMethodForKey: method contains all of that repetition that we've eliminated from the delegate method. This includes checking whether the unarchiver contains a key with a particular name before calling the corresponding method and passing in the value corresponding to that key.

Devices/MontyHall2/Classes/MontyHallViewController.m
```
-(void) invokeMethodForKey:(NSString *) keyName
             ifFoundIn:(NSKeyedUnarchiver *)unarchiver {
    if ([unarchiver containsValueForKey:keyName]) {
        [self performSelector:NSSelectorFromString(keyName)
                withObject:[NSNumber numberWithInt:[unarchiver
                                      decodeIntForKey:keyName]]];
    }
}
```

That's two variations on how we might handle data that specifies a method name and its argument. You may need to send very different types of data between devices, and you may want to format it in a variety of ways. Because you own both ends of the conversation, you can create any format you want when you send and consume it appropriately when you receive it. We'll look at another possible protocol later in this chapter.

11.7   Cleaning Up

Once the Contestant user has made their final selection, they will see whether they have won, and they will send their final selection to the MontyHall application so that the game show host can see whether the Contestant user has won. At this point, the game is over.

Neither Monty Hall nor the Contestant user has any further use for the connection between the two devices, so in the MontyHallViewController, we'll invoke the method disconnectFromAllPeers.

Devices/MontyHall2/Classes/MontyHallViewController.m

```
-(void) finalDoorSelected:(NSNumber *)doorNumberObject {
    NSUInteger doorNumber = [doorNumberObject intValue];
    [self setAllDoorsToHidden:YES];
    [self setDoorNumber:doorNumber toHidden:NO];
    if (doorNumber == prizeDoor) {
        self.statusField.text = @"The contestant wins.";
    } else {
        self.statusField.text = @"The contestant loses.";
    }
    [self.session disconnectFromAllPeers];
}
```

11.8   Advertising Peers

In this second example, we'll create a simple chat application and use the GKPeerPickerController class to advertise the availability of the application. You can see in the PeerChat1 directory that we have a view-based iPhone application with a single UITextField.[7]

The PeerChatViewController acts as the text field's UITextFieldDelegate. When the user enters their name, the application creates and starts up an instance of a GKPeerPickerController.

---

7.   This could have been an iPad application. Again, we've created an iPhone app because you need two devices to test this on.

We're going to set up the chat over Bluetooth by setting the peer picker controller's type mask to be GKPeerPickerConnectionTypeNearBy. When the devices are going to be near each other, say within 10 meters, Bluetooth is a good choice. You can also use WiFi, but then you have the potential problem that the devices are connected to different networks and won't see each other. Also, if you use WiFi, then you need to create your own interface to set up the Internet connection.

Here's how we create the GKPeerPickerController object and set the Peer-ChatViewController to be its delegate. We configure the peer picker connection to search over Bluetooth, and then we show the peer picker:

Devices/PeerChat1/Classes/PeerChatViewController.m

```
-(void)createAndStartPeerPicker {
    self.peerPC =[[GKPeerPickerController alloc] init];
    self.peerPC.delegate = self;
    self.peerPC.connectionTypesMask = GKPeerPickerConnectionTypeNearby;
    [self.peerPC show];
}
```

Next we'll use the peer picker controller to create and connect sessions.

11.9 Connecting Peers

We need to implement two delegate methods for the peer picker controller. The peerPickerController:sessionForConnectionType: method returns a session that we lazily initialize in the getter.[8]

The code should look pretty familiar. Except for the session mode being GKSessionModePeer instead of client or server, this is how we initialized the session earlier in this chapter:

Devices/PeerChat2/Classes/PeerChatViewController.m

```
-(GKSession *) session {
    if (!session) {
        self.session = [[GKSession alloc] initWithSessionID:@"example"
                                             displayName:self.userName
                                             sessionMode:GKSessionModePeer];
        self.session.delegate = self;
        [self.session setDataReceiveHandler:self withContext:nil];
    }
    return session;
}
```

In this case, we will now see other PeerChat instances looking to chat.

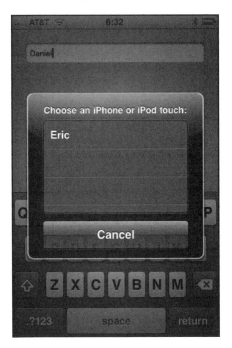

---

8. By *lazy initialization* we mean that we don't create it until it is needed.

Once one person selects another, the selected person's device will have a chance to respond.

All this happened because we returned a session in the preceding delegate method. Once a connection is made, we'll have to dismiss the peer picker controller and make sure that the session is set correctly. We do that in the following delegate method:

Devices/PeerChat2/Classes/PeerChatViewController.m

```
- (void)peerPickerController:(GKPeerPickerController *)picker
           didConnectPeer:(NSString *)peerID
                toSession:(GKSession *)activeSession {
    self.session = activeSession;
    [picker dismiss];
    self.peerPC = nil;
}
```

Now the two peers are connected and ready to communicate.

11.10 Chatting

In the PeerChat3 folder, you'll notice that we've added a UITextView and a corresponding property named chatView. When either user types a message into the text field, we'll display this message at the top of the text view and send the message to the connected peers. As before, we'll use the sendDataToAllPeers:withDataMode:error: method to send the data to the other devices. Because we are sending a string, we are able to encode it in place.

Devices/PeerChat3/Classes/PeerChatViewController.m

```objc
-(void) sendAllPeersMessage:(NSString *) message {
    [self.session sendDataToAllPeers:
                        [message dataUsingEncoding:NSUTF8StringEncoding]
                        withDataMode:GKSendDataReliable
                                error:nil];
}
```

Similarly, we need to use the data we receive from other peers.

Devices/PeerChat3/Classes/PeerChatViewController.m

```objc
- (void) receiveData: (NSData*) data
            fromPeer: (NSString*) peerID
           inSession: (GKSession*) session
             context: (void*) context {
    [self addMessage:[[[NSString alloc] initWithData:data
                                            encoding:NSUTF8StringEncoding]
                        autorelease]
        forParticipant:[self.session displayNameForPeer:peerID]];
}
```

Finally, if one of the peers disconnects, we will need to communicate that fact to the other peers. We'll implement that here:

Devices/PeerChat3/Classes/PeerChatViewController.m

```objc
- (void)session:(GKSession *)session
           peer:(NSString *)peerID
 didChangeState:(GKPeerConnectionState)state {
    switch (state) {
        case GKPeerStateDisconnected:
            [self addMessage:@"*** has disconnected"
              forParticipant:[self.session displayNameForPeer:peerID]];
            //handle services disconnecting
            break;
        default:
            break;
    }
}
```

This is a fairly bare-bones chat application, but it has allowed us to look at setting up and using peer devices.

11.11 Summary

This chapter has been full of many cool techniques, but what does it have to do with you? Actually, that's a very important question to ask yourself even if you're not creating an application where the use of these techniques is immediately obvious.

At one point, iTunes was just an application for buying, burning, and listening to your music. Then this music application became Bonjour-aware, and suddenly iTunes has the ability to share your music and to discover and listen to other people's music.

In this chapter, we showed you two different strategies for discovering nearby devices that are running the same application you are. You've learned how to move data between these other devices and yours. The techniques are not simple, but on the other hand, they are not overly complicated. You should always consider how your app might become richer if it could discover one or more nearby instances of the same app running on another iPhone or iPad.

Chapter 12

Working with Documents

There's been a progression in how you work with documents on Apple's handheld devices. The iPod was meant for consuming media and documents produced elsewhere. You could listen to music, watch videos, and view your calendar and addresses on the iPod, but you couldn't make any changes to your appointments or contact information.

The iPhone and iPod touch changed this. You can write text messages and email and create new content on them. Even though it is possible to author content on these devices, their primary use case is still the consumption of content produced elsewhere.

The iPad extends this spectrum. It is big enough to be used to author documents. Apple made this distinction clear by releasing iPad versions of Pages, Numbers, and Keynote on the day the iPad shipped. You can see from these iWork applications how Apple imagines you will work with documents on the iPad.

In this chapter, we'll look at several aspects of working with documents. You'll learn how to enable the transfer of documents to and from your application's Documents directory using iTunes. You'll open and save documents in that directory. You'll register your application as being able to open a particular document type, and you'll use the UIDocumentInteractionController class and its delegate to let other applications open documents that your application cannot open. Finally, you'll learn how to preview documents.

For better or worse, the iPad doesn't have a Finder. Your users should not be thinking about directory structure. They shouldn't worry about where a document is stored. They just want to work with the document. We're going to make that easy for them.

12.1 Transferring Documents Using iTunes

In Section 6.6, *Saving Our Drawing as a PDF*, on page 118, we drew our warning symbol in a PDF file that we saved in the Documents directory. Each application has its own Documents directory, and until iPhoneOS 3.2, the contents of this directory were invisible to the user. With a simple addition to the application plist, you'll be able to transfer files to and from this directory from your host computer using iTunes.

Open the version of the Bezier project that we used to write the PDF. You should find this in the code download in the /code/Drawing/Bezier12/ directory. Open Bezier-Info.plist with a text editor, and add the following key-value pair to the dictionary:

```
<key>UIFileSharingEnabled</key>
<true/>
```

If you prefer, you can double-click the plist and use the plist editor to add the entry. The corresponding phrase in the drop down list is Application supports iTunes file sharing.

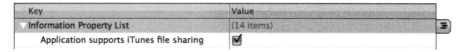

Key	Value	
▼ Information Property List	(14 items)	☰
Application supports iTunes file sharing	☑	

If the Bezier app is already on your device, delete it so that our new settings will be picked up when we sync in iTunes.

Now build and run with the device as the target. Once you have run the app on the device, quit the app and sync your iPad using iTunes. When you're device is selected, on the bottom on the Apps tab you should see something like Figure 12.1, on the next page.

That's all it takes to enable document transfers between your computer and your iPad.[1] The documents you add will be stored in the top level of the application's Documents directory.

Save Warning.pdf to your computer by dragging it out of iTunes, and then open it. You'll see the warning symbol we drew on the iPad. You can add files to the iPad from your computer, but it won't do us any good. The Bezier app doesn't know how to open any files. Let's modify the Feelings app from Chapter 5, *Custom Keyboards*, on page 93.

---

1. You can also transfer files over the network using Bonjour, email documents to yourself, and open them on your iPad or download them in Safari. Those details are beyond the scope of this book.

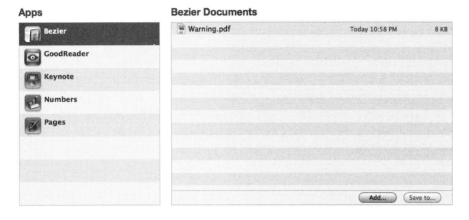

Figure 12.1: YOUR APPLICATION'S DOCUMENTS SHOW UP IN iTUNES.

12.2 Persisting Documents

In our Feelings app, we were able to type text and emoticons into a text view. In that example, when we quit the application and relaunched it, we started with a blank slate. In most useful applications, you're going to want to save your work so that when you relaunch, you can continue from where you were the last time.[2]

On the iPad, you do this just as you would on any other computer. You need to specify the path to the document location, and you'll need a way to read from files and write to files. What changes on the iPad from other environments in which you've enabled this sort of functionality are the expectations of your users. On the iPad, as the user types new text into a document, they don't expect that they'll have to manually save the document from time to time. They expect that you'll take care of it for them.

In the Feelings app, you may want to save the user's work whenever they dismiss the keyboard. That act says, "I'm done editing for now." You also may want to save their work when they quit the application.

---

2. If you're working with multiple documents, you'll need to present a gallery or some way for the user to select the document they want or to create a new one, but the rest of the details are unchanged.

Think of it from the user's point of view. They start up your app, type something into the text view, and now, since they are finished, they hit the Home button and quit your app. They probably expect their work to be saved.

Open the version of the Feelings project in /code/Files/Feelings7. You'll see that we've added a new class to manage the saving and opening of files named MyFileManager and set it to be the text view's delegate. When the text view resigns the first responder, textViewShouldEndEditing: is called.[3] When the application terminates, the app delegate calls the applicationWillTerminate: method. In either case, the MyFileManager object saves the current document.

Files/Feelings7/Classes/MyFileManager.m

```
-(void) saveDocument:(UITextView *) textView {
    NSError *error1 = nil;
    [textView.text writeToFile:[self fileLocation]
                    atomically:YES
                      encoding:NSUTF8StringEncoding
                         error:&error1];
}
- (BOOL)textViewShouldEndEditing:(UITextView *)textView {
    [self saveDocument:textView];
    return YES;
}
-(void)applicationWillTerminate:(UITextView *)textView{
    [self saveDocument:textView];
}
```

Also, when the application first starts up, the app delegate calls the applicationDidFinishLaunching: method, which loads the Mood.txt file if it exists and displays its contents in the text view.

Files/Feelings7/Classes/MyFileManager.m

```
-(void)applicationDidFinishLaunching:(UITextView *) textView {
    NSError *error2;
    if ([[NSFileManager defaultManager] fileExistsAtPath:[self fileLocation]] ) {
        textView.text = [NSString stringWithContentsOfFile:[self fileLocation]
                                          encoding:NSUTF8StringEncoding
                                             error:&error2 ];
    }
}
```

---

3. Recall that when the text field is selected, it becomes the first responder and is ready for keyboard input, so the keyboard appears. When you are no longer interested in providing input for the text field, it should resign the first responder so that the keyboard is dismissed.

We now have an application that can work with plain-text files. Suppose we write another app and provide it with a text file that needs to be read. We'd like to allow the Feelings app to help. There are three steps:

1. We're going to let the system know that the Feelings app can handle plain-text content. We'll do that with a simple addition to the plist.

2. We'll modify the Feelings app so that it opens the plain-text file that is being handed off to it.

3. We'll provide our new application with the ability to ask for help when it encounters a file type that it can't open itself.

We'll take these one at a time.

12.3 Registering File Types

Our first step is to register with the system that Feelings is able to open plain-text documents. You can add this entry to Feelings-Info.plist in a text editor or using the plist editor.

```
<key>CFBundleDocumentTypes</key>
<array>
    <dict>
        <key>LSItemContentTypes</key>
        <array>
            <string>public.plain-text</string>
        </array>
    </dict>
</array>
```

Notice that the value corresponding to the CFBundleDocumentTypes key is an array of dictionaries. Each dictionary is used to specify a document type that the application can open. Here we specify the plain-text type using the Uniform Type Identifier (UTI).[4] We've used only the LSItemContentTypes key. We could also have used the key CFBundleTypeIconFiles to pass in PNG files to use for the file icons. If you are going to create your own custom types, you should consult Apple's *iPad Programming Guide* [App10b].

Remove the existing version of the Feelings app from your iPad, and build and run the app with the device as the target. Feelings should

---

4. http://developer.apple.com/iphone/library/documentation/FileManagement/Conceptual/
understanding_utis/understand_utis_intro/understand_utis_intro.html

launch as before. You shouldn't notice anything different about it. We haven't changed the way Feelings works in any way—we have changed how other applications view Feelings.

To see this change, create a plain-text file using TextEdit and email it to yourself as an attachment. Check your mail on your iPad, and select the attachment. Mail should take you to a view like this with an Open In... button in the top-right corner. Select the button, and you should see something like this:

Those are the apps that have registered with the system that they can open plain-text files. You may have a different list on your system depending on what apps you have installed. You should, however, now see the Feelings app in the list. That's step 1.

Once we take step 2, you'll be able to view the text file with the Feelings app. For now, the Feelings app will open with whatever its Mood.txt file contained when you last ran the app.

12.4 Opening a File at Launch

When the user chooses to open the file with the Feelings app, the file to open and a dictionary are passed to the app. We use this information inside the application:didFinishLaunchingWithOptions: method in the FeelingsAppDelegate.

This may be the first time you've ever worked with any options when this method is called. Apple is clear that if the application launches because there is a file to be opened, then you need to open that file right away and display it to the user.

Files/Feelings9/Classes/FeelingsAppDelegate.m

```
- (BOOL)application:(UIApplication *)application
        didFinishLaunchingWithOptions:(NSDictionary *)launchOptions {
    [self.window addSubview:self.viewController.view];
    [self.window makeKeyAndVisible];
```

```
▶          [self.myFM applicationDidFinishLaunchingWithFileURL:
▶                  [launchOptions valueForKey:UIApplicationLaunchOptionsURLKey]
▶              inTextView:self.viewController.textView];
           return YES;
}
```

Here we're reading the NSURL corresponding to the document to be opened from the options dictionary. If we wanted to call back to the calling application at some point, we can pull its bundle ID from the UIApplicationLaunchOptionsSourceApplicationKey. If there is more information that needs to be passed along, it can be included as entries in a dictionary corresponding to the key UIApplicationLaunchOptionsAnnotationKey.

In our case, we might do something like this in the MyFileManager class:

`Files/Feelings9/Classes/MyFileManager.m`

```
-(void)applicationDidFinishLaunchingWithFileURL:(NSURL *)fileURL
                                     inTextView:(UITextView *) textView {
    NSError *error2;
        textView.text = [NSString stringWithContentsOfURL: fileURL
                                       encoding:NSUTF8StringEncoding
                                          error:&error2 ];
}
```

We should, of course, check the error and display it at least during development. The point here is that we are opening the file that is passed in to us by the system when this app received the request to open this file.[5]

Build and run, and then quit the Feelings app. Now try to open the plain-text document from Mail using the Feelings app. The Mail app should quit, and the Feelings app should launch and display the contents of the text file in the text view.

12.5 Opening Files

Whenever your application encounters a file type it can't handle itself, you should provide an instance of a UIDocumentInteractionController. That's how the Mail app knew how to offer the option to the user of opening the text document with the Feelings app. Let's create a simple app that will do nothing but ask other apps for help working with a document.

---

5. Notice the code to save the document has also been removed because it's no longer part of what's being illustrated.

Create a new view-based iPad app named SingleFile. Add the following
to SingleFile-Info.plist to allow syncing using iTunes:

```
<key>UIFileSharingEnabled</key>
<true/>
```

Build and run on the device. Quit SingleFile, and sync your iPad. You
should now be able to add a file to SingleFile in iTunes. Add the text
document that you created before. We'll use the name Mood.txt in the
book, but you can use another name if you prefer.

When the SingleFile application launches, we want to open the Mood.txt
file. Unfortunately, SingleFile doesn't have a clue what to do with a
plain-text document. It needs help, and that's where the UIDocumentInteractionController comes in. We use one for each document. Declare
a property of type UIDocumentInteractionController in the view controller
header file:

Files/SingleFile1/Classes/SingleFileViewController.h

```
#import <UIKit/UIKit.h>

@interface SingleFileViewController : UIViewController {
}
@property (nonatomic, retain) UIDocumentInteractionController *controller;
-(void)applicationDidFinishLaunching;

@end
```

We've also declared the method applicationDidFinishLaunching:, which you
should call from the end of the app delegate's application:didFinishLaunch-
ingWithOptions: method.

We'll lazy initialize the controller in the getter.

Files/SingleFile1/Classes/SingleFileViewController.m

```
-(UIDocumentInteractionController *) controller {
    if (controller == nil) {
        NSString *applicationDocumentsDirectory =
                [NSSearchPathForDirectoriesInDomains(NSDocumentDirectory,
                                                     NSUserDomainMask,
                                                     YES)     lastObject];
        NSString *fileLocation =
        [applicationDocumentsDirectory stringByAppendingPathComponent:@"Mood.txt"]
        NSURL *fileURL = [NSURL fileURLWithPath:fileLocation];
        self.controller =
            [UIDocumentInteractionController interactionControllerWithURL:fileURL
    }
    return controller;
}
```

Most of the code creates the URL for Mood.txt. If your text file has a different name, you'll need to use that in place of Mood.txt here. We initialize the controller with the class method interactionControllerWithURL.

Now that we have our UIDocumentInteractionController, there are three basic things we can use it for: present the user with a popover containing the applications that are available to open the file, preview the document in a modal view controller, and present the options of what can be done (open or preview).

Only those options that are available are presented. So, for example, in our current application, we are going to present a popover for opening Mood.txt. If no application is available that has announced the capabilities of opening a plain-text file, then the popover will not be displayed.

Here's where we display the popover for opening Mood.txt:

Files/SingleFile1/Classes/SingleFileViewController.m

```
-(void)applicationDidFinishLaunching {
    [self.controller presentOpenInMenuFromRect:CGRectMake(200, 200, 200, 200)
                                        inView:self.view
                                      animated:YES];
}
```

Build and run SingleFile on the device, and you will see this popover when the app launches:

Open the file in Feelings. SingleFile will quit, and Feelings will launch with your document displayed.[6]

---

6. You can select the text field to edit the document, but at this point we aren't saving any of the changes.

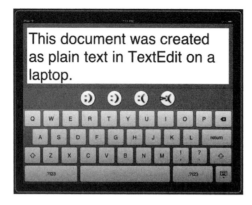

You can follow these steps on the simulator as well. Build and run Feelings on the simulator, and then quit the app. Build and run SingleFile as well. At this point, nothing should happen. You can't add the Mood.txt file to the simulator using iTunes, but you can add it directly to the Documents directory in ~/Library/Application\ Support/iPhone\ Simulator/3.2/Applications. Build and run, and you should see the popover that we saw on the device.

Now copy a PDF into the directory. For example, we could use the PDF for this book if you have it. Name it iPadBook.pdf, and change the controller method to load this file instead of Mood.txt. This time when you build and run, no popover appears. There is no application on your device that has registered to open PDFs.

12.6 Previewing Files

We can't open the PDF, but we can preview it without leaving the Single-File application. We need to change the call to presentOpenInMenuFromRect:inView:animated: to presentPreviewAnimated:.

```
Files/SingleFile2/Classes/SingleFileViewController.m
-(void)applicationDidFinishLaunching {
    self.controller.delegate = self;
    [self.controller presentPreviewAnimated:YES];
}
```

You can see that we also need to set the delegate for the UIDocumentInteractionController. We didn't need to do this when we were opening a document, but when we preview a document, we need to specify the view controller that will be the parent for the modal view being displayed.

We do that in this delegate method:

`Files/SingleFile2/Classes/SingleFileViewController.m`

```
- (UIViewController *)documentInteractionControllerViewControllerForPreview:
                            (UIDocumentInteractionController *)controller
{
    return self;
}
```

Add the declaration of the UIDocumentInteractionControllerDelegate proto-col to the header file. Build and run. You should see a full preview of the PDF.

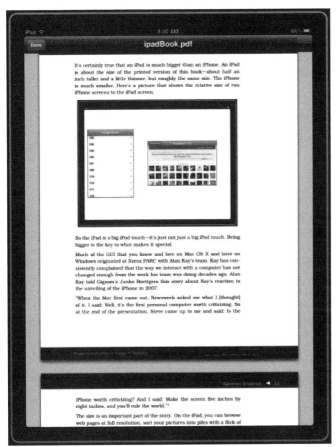

12.7   Summary

Remember that a big part of the magic of the iPad is that it stays out of our end user's way. The techniques in this chapter make it easier for your users to move their documents between your application and their computer without knowing anything about a file system. You've learned how to get your application to cooperate with other applications to preview or open different document types.

iPad applications tend to be a little more complex than iPhone applications and less complex than Mac OS X applications. When you write for the iPad, you might find it more appropriate to build a suite of smaller applications rather than one big, complex one. The techniques in this chapter make it easy for you to pass documents back and forth depending on what the user needs to do.

Chapter 13

Putting It All Together

Congratulations. You've delved into a lot of nooks and crannies of iPad programming while exploring the discrete topics presented in this book. We covered a wide range of iPad topics from split-view controllers to targeting external displays—from the new gesture APIs to getting your devices to communicate with each other. Although everything we've covered in this book was introduced for the iPhone 3.2 SDKs for the iPad, you'll find many of them in iOS 4 for the iPhone as well. Most of the techniques you've learned in this book apply both to the iPad and to the latest version of the iPhone and iPod touch.

Throughout this book we've focused on showing you *how* to do stuff at the technical level—how to show a movie, how to use a popover control, and the like. Now let's take a step back and look at things from a higher level. This chapter contains our top-ten list of things to keep in mind when building iPad applications.

We'll finish this chapter and the book by thanking some of the many people who helped us with this project.

13.1 Start with the User

Before you write a line of code or create your first nib, you need to have a clear idea of who your app is for. Apple's recommendation for iPhone apps is that you create a clear and concise product description. This advice is just as important for iPad apps.

Know who your target audience is and what specific task your app is designed to perform. This will help you identify features that need to be included and—just as important—which features you should leave out. A solid view of your user will help you determine whether you are creating a universal app, an iPad-only app, or two apps: one for the iPhone and one for the iPad.

Feature creep is easy without a clear idea of your user and the problem you are solving for them. Someone will beta test your app and say something like, "You know, it would be cool if you would just add...." The feature they suggest may be easy to add and might be as cool as your friend suggests. But if it doesn't fit into the core description of what the app does, it can make your app harder to use and less appealing to your target audience.

13.2 Treat Landscape and Portrait Views with Equal Importance

Pick up the iPhone with one hand. Whether you're holding it to your ear to make a phone call or looking up something in a table view, you are probably holding it in portrait mode. Portrait is the preferred orientation on the iPhone—at least for now.

The iPad is completely different. There is no natural orientation for the device. Sure, there's a single Home button, but there's nothing to encourage the users to operate the device with the button on the bottom. Also, some of the cases force a default landscape orientation with the Home button along the left side.

You need to support both portrait and landscape modes in your application. You need to allow the user to start your app in either orientation, and you need to make the most out of whichever orientation they choose to use.

13.3 Flatten the Hierarchy

You have probably built up a bag of tricks from writing iPhone apps. These were good tricks for the phone, but you now need to reconsider some of your design decisions. A fundamental compromise you needed to make when targeting the phone was deep hierarchies. Your phone can display only a small amount of data at once, so you learned to use tab bars and nav controllers and helped the user move from screen to screen to navigate down to the level of detail that they need.

Technically, all of these techniques still work on the iPad. But stop and reconsider your app from a design and usability standpoint. You can now display more information at once on a single screen in a way that is more easily understood by your user.

We saw an example of replacing a navigation controller for iPhone with a split view on the iPad. In the iPhone version, the user selected a row, and the detail view replaced the table view. If the user wanted to go back and see what other choices are available, they had to hit the Back button on the detail view to return to the table view.

On the iPad, we could use the split view to display the table view on the left side and the detail view in the rest of the screen. The user could make a choice and see the detail view without losing sight of their other choices. Even in portrait view these choices are in a popover that the user can bring up with the touch of a button without losing the current detail view. Look to flatten the hierarchy in your application as well.

13.4 Create Immersive, Rich, Realistic Views

If you were an Apple developer before the arrival of the iPad, you know that Apple's recommendation has typically been to stick to the Apple UI guidelines, using standard UI components and creating custom views only in extreme cases.

Those recommendations have changed with the iPad, and Apple is now encouraging you to build interfaces that are based on real-world realism. You only have to look as far as iBooks, the calendar, and many third-party applications to see great examples. When you design your applications, consider creating views that reflect your application's real-world counterpart (assuming there is one). Employ a designer if needed. This isn't to say that you shouldn't use standard components where they make sense: these will help your users navigate your application.

13.5 Gestures Are Powerful

With iOS 3.2 (and 4.0 on the iPhone), Apple has given us a powerful new API for easily adding common gestures such as taps, pans, pinches, holds, rotations, and swipes. Study these carefully, and make sure you are using them in a manner that is expected by your users (*Apple iPad Human Interface Guidelines* [App10a]); the last thing you want to do is make your users use gestures in a unconventional, confusing way.

That said, Apple's new APIs also give you the power to create your own unique gestures, and although these should be used sparingly, the vocabulary of gestures is still evolving. Who's to say you won't invent the next new gesture or at least a new one that makes sense for your unique application?

13.6 Your iPad Wants to Collaborate

At some point during your development cycle, ask yourself, "What changes if my stand-alone application could communicate with other nearby instances of the same application?" Perhaps an application that you've designed to allow people to create documents becomes an application that also allows people to collaborate on a document. Perhaps an app that you've designed to allow people to record their ideas becomes an app that also allows people to share and compare ideas.

You've seen in this book that the mechanism of communicating between devices is pretty straightforward. You decide whether the relationship between instances is client-server or a collection of peers, and then you respond to delegate methods. The business decisions are the difficult ones. What do you want to be able to accomplish by collaborating? The possibilities are endless.

13.7 Docs

You have an iPhone, an iPad, and a laptop—how hard should it be to get a document you've created on one device onto another device? It turns out, with the iPhone 3.2 SDK, the answer is "Not that hard." You can easily support moving documents from one device to another any time you sync during iTunes.

We also looked at how we build an ecosystem of applications that know how to handle different document types. You saw how easy it was to let the system know that your application can support certain types of documents and how to enable your document to use the help of other applications to open documents that your app doesn't support.

13.8 Video Matters

If video makes sense in your application, then you now have the tools to build compelling experiences with video embedded directly into your views. Beyond that, the video APIs give you all the functionality you need to synchronize your interface to the video, and vice versa. Think about taking video beyond the "video in a web page" model, and explore true interactive experiences including bonus information, social features, and shared viewing experiences (for starters).

13.9 External Displays Require a Custom Implementation

As much as you'd like to just plug your iPad into an external monitor and have the display mirrored, that isn't how the iPad works; to display content on the second screen, you need to create and manage a separate view hierarchy.

Although this may seem like a pain, it can be used to your advantage. Consider routing the video in your sports application to the big screen while using the iPad to switch between camera angles and to monitor the game statistics. Or, play the moderator of a game show where puzzles are displayed on the large screen while you run the game from your iPad. Get creative with your second screen!

13.10 Improve Your Quality of Service with Streaming Video

For your video application, you'll also need to consider whether video can be included directly into your bundle or needs to be streamed to your application. If the answer is streaming, then you'll need to nail down the details of segmenting and hosting to support Apple's HLS protocol, particularly if you are delivering high-value or high-quality content.

There's a learning curve to preparing content for HLS, but it is worth the effort given your video player will adapt to the available bandwidth, even if it changes over time.

13.11 Acknowledgments

This book has been a lot of fun for both of us.

We both thank the tech reviewers and readers who submitted errata. The feedback was so helpful. In particular, thanks to Kim Shrier who bought the beta and provided us with excellent suggestions throughout the beta process. Janine Sisk gave us detailed suggestions during tech review that improved this final version immensely. Carlos A. Weber, MD, and Paul Lynch gave excellent technical reviews, and Elisabeth Robson and Joe Heck also helped the quality of the book.

Also, thanks to Chris Adamson and Craig Castelaz, two friends who are always willing to chat about Obj-C code. Thanks as well to Bill Dudney and Eryk Vershen who provided valuable help on technical points.

From Daniel

Thanks first to my coauthor, Eric Freeman. Eric and I have known each other for a long time and worked on projects here and there but never on a book together. He was amazingly easy to work with, and even though we mainly wrote separate chapters, this was a very collaborative project. I look forward to working on another book with Eric sometime.

Thanks to Mike and Nicole Clark, owners of the Pragmatic Studio (http://pragmaticstudio.com). I've learned so much in the past few years by teaching classes on programming the Mac, the iPhone, and now the iPad. I'm currently coteaching public classes with Matt Drance and initially cotaught these classes with Bill Dudney. These guys are both rock stars who have taught me so much (in fact, Bill has taken the evangelist position at Apple that Matt left).

Thanks to Kimmy-the-wonderwife who continues to be the best. Spending time with Kim and our daughter, Maggie, are my favorite parts of every day. My writing companion was Anabelle, our $2\frac{1}{2}$-year-old German Shorthair/Black Lab mix. She looks over my shoulder as I sit in the backyard at the picnic table typing code and prose. When she looks away, I realize I've lost her attention, and I rewrite that paragraph.

Finally, thanks to my friends and colleagues at the Prags. It's been my home for four years, and I've enjoyed editing and writing books with this team. I'll miss working with them.

You can keep up with my latest projects at http://dimsumthinking.com.

From Eric

A big thanks to my coauthor, Daniel Steinberg. I've always wanted to do a project with Dan, and I'm glad we found such an exciting project to work on together. I also want to thank Dan for dragging me back into Cocoa programming, I've never had so much fun. I'm looking forward to more projects and spin-offs in the future.

Thanks as well to my new friends at Prags, Dave Thomas and Andy Hunt. I've never seen such an easy and powerful publishing tool set, and I really enjoyed the process of creating a book using them. A special thanks to Dave as well for jumping in when we needed a bit of extra help on the editor side.

A special thanks to my amazing wife, Jenn Freeman, who carried our child during the writing of this book and gave birth just two weeks before it was finished. Avary Katherine Freeman often slept nearby as I put the finishing touches on chapters.

Finally, thanks to you, the reader, for picking up this book and joining us in learning how to write experiences on these amazing devices.

Please visit me at http://ericfreeman.com.

Appendix A

Bibliography

[App09a]   Apple, Inc.   *HTTP Live Streaming Overview.*   http:
           //developer.apple.com/iphone/library/documentation/
           NetworkingInternet/Conceptual/StreamingMediaGuide/, 2009.

[App09b]   Apple, Inc.   *iPhone Application Programming Guide.*
           http://developer.apple.com/iphone/library/documentation/
           iPhone/Conceptual/iPhoneOSProgrammingGuide, 2009.

[App10a]   Apple, Inc.   *Apple iPad Human Interfaces Guidelines.*
           http://developer.apple.com/iphone/library/documentation/
           General/Conceptual/iPadHIG/Introduction/Introduction.html,
           2010.

[App10b]   Apple, Inc. *iPad Programming Guide.* {http://developer.apple.
           com/iphone/library/documentation/General/Conceptual/iP
           adProgrammingGuide/Introduction/Introduction.html,
           2010.

[App10c]   Apple, Inc. *MPMoviePlayerController Class Reference.* https://
           developer.apple.com/iphone/prerelease/library/documentation/
           MediaPlayer/Reference/MPMoviePlayerController_Class/
           MPMoviePlayerController/MPMoviePlayerController.html, 2010.

[DA09]   Bill Dudney and Chris Adamson. *iPhone SDK Development.*
           The Pragmatic Programmers, LLC, Raleigh, NC, and Dallas,
           TX, 2009.

[Dud08]   Bill Dudney. *Core Animation for OS X: Creating Dynamic Compelling User Interfaces*. The Pragmatic Programmers, LLC, Raleigh, NC, and Dallas, TX, 2008.

[GL06]   David Gelphman and Bunny Laden. *Programming with Quartz, 2D and PDF Graphics in Mac OS X*. Morgan Kaufman, San Francisco, 2006.

[Ste09]   Daniel H Steinberg. *Cocoa Programming: A Quick-Start Guide for Developers*. The Pragmatic Programmers, LLC, Raleigh, NC, and Dallas, TX, 2009.

[Tho06]   R. Scott Thompson. *Quartz 2D graphics for Mac OS X developers*. Pearson Education, Inc., Boston, MA, 2006.

Index

Where to Go From Here

We've got the paperback books, eBooks and screencasts you want for Mac development at PragProg.com. From Cocoa to Core Data, Core Animation, iPhone and Xcode, we've got what you need. Visit our Mac page at http://www.pragprog.com/categories/mac.

Cocoa Programming

Cocoa Programming shows you how to get productive with Cocoa–fast! You'll learn to use the Apple developer tools to design your user interface, write the code, and create the data model. We'll show you Objective-C concepts when you are ready to apply them throughout the book. By the end of the book, you'll be a Cocoa programmer.

Cocoa Programming: A Quick-Start Guide for Developers
Daniel H Steinberg
(450 pages) ISBN: 978-19343563-0-2. $32.95
http://pragprog.com/titles/dscpq

Core Data

Learn the Apple Core Data APIs from the ground up. You can concentrate on designing the model for your application, and use the power of Core Data to do the rest. This book will take you from beginning with Core Data through to expert level configurations that you will not find anywhere else. Learn why you should be using Core Data for your next Cocoa project, and how to use it most effectively.

Core Data: Apple's API for Persisting Data under Mac OS X
Marcus S. Zarra
(256 pages) ISBN: 978-1-93435-632-6. $32.95
http://pragprog.com/titles/mzcd

The Pragmatic Bookshelf

The Pragmatic Bookshelf features books written by developers for developers. The titles continue the well-known Pragmatic Programmer style and continue to garner awards and rave reviews. As development gets more and more difficult, the Pragmatic Programmers will be there with more titles and products to help you stay on top of your game.

Visit Us Online

Home page for iPad Programming
http://pragprog.com/titles/sfipad
Source code from this book, errata, and other resources. Come give us feedback, too!

Register for Updates
http://pragprog.com/updates
Be notified when updates and new books become available.

Join the Community
http://pragprog.com/community
Read our weblogs, join our online discussions, participate in our mailing list, interact with our wiki, and benefit from the experience of other Pragmatic Programmers.

New and Noteworthy
http://pragprog.com/news
Check out the latest pragmatic developments, new titles and other offerings.

Save on the eBook

Save on the eBook versions of this title. Owning the paper version of this book entitles you to purchase the electronic versions at a terrific discount.

PDFs are great for carrying around on your laptop—they are hyperlinked, have color, and are fully searchable. Most titles are also available for the iPhone and iPod touch, Amazon Kindle, and other popular e-book readers.

Buy now at pragprog.com/coupon.

Contact Us

Online Orders:	www.pragprog.com/catalog
Customer Service:	support@pragprog.com
Non-English Versions:	translations@pragprog.com
Pragmatic Teaching:	academic@pragprog.com
Author Proposals:	proposals@pragprog.com
Contact us:	1-800-699-PROG (+1 919 847 3884)